# The works of the Right Reverend Jonathan Shipley, D.D. ... In two volumes. ... Volume 2 of 2

Jonathan Shipley

*The works of the Right Reverend Jonathan Shipley, D.D. ... In two volumes. ... Volume 2 of 2*
Shipley, Jonathan
ESTCID: T094718
Reproduction from British Library

London : printed for T. Cadell, 1792.
2v.,plate : port. ; 8°

Eighteenth Century
Collections Online
Print Editions

## Gale ECCO Print Editions

Relive history with *Eighteenth Century Collections Online*, now available in print for the independent historian and collector. This series includes the most significant English-language and foreign-language works printed in Great Britain during the eighteenth century, and is organized in seven different subject areas including literature and language; medicine, science, and technology; and religion and philosophy. The collection also includes thousands of important works from the Americas.

The eighteenth century has been called "The Age of Enlightenment." It was a period of rapid advance in print culture and publishing, in world exploration, and in the rapid growth of science and technology – all of which had a profound impact on the political and cultural landscape. At the end of the century the American Revolution, French Revolution and Industrial Revolution, perhaps three of the most significant events in modern history, set in motion developments that eventually dominated world political, economic, and social life.

In a groundbreaking effort, Gale initiated a revolution of its own: digitization of epic proportions to preserve these invaluable works in the largest online archive of its kind. Contributions from major world libraries constitute over 175,000 original printed works. Scanned images of the actual pages, rather than transcriptions, recreate the works *as they first appeared.*

Now for the first time, these high-quality digital scans of original works are available via print-on-demand, making them readily accessible to libraries, students, independent scholars, and readers of all ages.

For our initial release we have created seven robust collections to form one the world's most comprehensive catalogs of $18^{th}$ century works.

*Initial Gale ECCO Print Editions collections include:*

> ### *History and Geography*
> Rich in titles on English life and social history, this collection spans the world as it was known to eighteenth-century historians and explorers. Titles include a wealth of travel accounts and diaries, histories of nations from throughout the world, and maps and charts of a world that was still being discovered. Students of the War of American Independence will find fascinating accounts from the British side of conflict.

*Social Science*
Delve into what it was like to live during the eighteenth century by reading the first-hand accounts of everyday people, including city dwellers and farmers, businessmen and bankers, artisans and merchants, artists and their patrons, politicians and their constituents. Original texts make the American, French, and Industrial revolutions vividly contemporary.

*Medicine, Science and Technology*
Medical theory and practice of the 1700s developed rapidly, as is evidenced by the extensive collection, which includes descriptions of diseases, their conditions, and treatments. Books on science and technology, agriculture, military technology, natural philosophy, even cookbooks, are all contained here.

*Literature and Language*
Western literary study flows out of eighteenth-century works by Alexander Pope, Daniel Defoe, Henry Fielding, Frances Burney, Denis Diderot, Johann Gottfried Herder, Johann Wolfgang von Goethe, and others. Experience the birth of the modern novel, or compare the development of language using dictionaries and grammar discourses.

*Religion and Philosophy*
The Age of Enlightenment profoundly enriched religious and philosophical understanding and continues to influence present-day thinking. Works collected here include masterpieces by David Hume, Immanuel Kant, and Jean-Jacques Rousseau, as well as religious sermons and moral debates on the issues of the day, such as the slave trade. The Age of Reason saw conflict between Protestantism and Catholicism transformed into one between faith and logic -- a debate that continues in the twenty-first century.

*Law and Reference*
This collection reveals the history of English common law and Empire law in a vastly changing world of British expansion. Dominating the legal field is the *Commentaries of the Law of England* by Sir William Blackstone, which first appeared in 1765. Reference works such as almanacs and catalogues continue to educate us by revealing the day-to-day workings of society.

*Fine Arts*
The eighteenth-century fascination with Greek and Roman antiquity followed the systematic excavation of the ruins at Pompeii and Herculaneum in southern Italy; and after 1750 a neoclassical style dominated all artistic fields. The titles here trace developments in mostly English-language works on painting, sculpture, architecture, music, theater, and other disciplines. Instructional works on musical instruments, catalogs of art objects, comic operas, and more are also included.

bibliolife
old books. new life.

## The BiblioLife Network

This project was made possible in part by the BiblioLife Network (BLN), a project aimed at addressing some of the huge challenges facing book preservationists around the world. The BLN includes libraries, library networks, archives, subject matter experts, online communities and library service providers. We believe every book ever published should be available as a high-quality print reproduction; printed on-demand anywhere in the world. This insures the ongoing accessibility of the content and helps generate sustainable revenue for the libraries and organizations that work to preserve these important materials.

The following book is in the "public domain" and represents an authentic reproduction of the text as printed by the original publisher. While we have attempted to accurately maintain the integrity of the original work, there are sometimes problems with the original work or the micro-film from which the books were digitized. This can result in minor errors in reproduction. Possible imperfections include missing and blurred pages, poor pictures, markings and other reproduction issues beyond our control. Because this work is culturally important, we have made it available as part of our commitment to protecting, preserving, and promoting the world's literature.

## GUIDE TO FOLD-OUTS MAPS and OVERSIZED IMAGES

The book you are reading was digitized from microfilm captured over the past thirty to forty years. Years after the creation of the original microfilm, the book was converted to digital files and made available in an online database.

In an online database, page images do not need to conform to the size restrictions found in a printed book. When converting these images back into a printed bound book, the page sizes are standardized in ways that maintain the detail of the original. For large images, such as fold-out maps, the original page image is split into two or more pages

Guidelines used to determine how to split the page image follows:

• Some images are split vertically; large images require vertical and horizontal splits.
• For horizontal splits, the content is split left to right.
• For vertical splits, the content is split from top to bottom.
• For both vertical and horizontal splits, the image is processed from top left to bottom right.

156

# THE
# WORKS
OF

THE RIGHT REVEREND

*JONATHAN SHIPLEY,* D.D.

LORD BISHOP OF ST. ASAPH.

# THE
# WORKS
## OF
### THE RIGHT REVEREND
## *JONATHAN SHIPLEY*, D. D.
### LORD BISHOP OF ST. ASAPH.

IN TWO VOLUMES,

VOL. II.

LONDON:
PRINTED FOR T. CADELL, IN THE STRAND.
M,DCC,XCII.

# CONTENTS.

## A CHARGE

*Delivered to the Clergy of the Diocese of St. Asaph, at the Primary Visitation in 1770,* - - 1

## CHARGE II.

*Delivered in the year 1774,* - 25

*Address to the Reader,* - - 51

## CHARGE III.

*Delivered in the year 1788,* - 65

## CHARGE IV.

*Delivered in the year 1782,* - 121

## A SPEECH

*Intended to have been spoken on the Bill for altering the Charters of the Colony of Massachusett's Bay,* - - 159

## A SPEECH

*On the Appeal from a Decree in the Court of Chancery, in favour of Literary Property, in the year 1774,* 201

## A SPEECH

*On the Bill for repealing the Penal Laws against Protestant Dissenters, in the year 1779,* - - 234

# CONTENTS.

### SERMON

*Preached before the House of Lords, in the abbey church of St. Peter, Westminster, on* Tuesday, January 30, 1770, *being the day appointed to be observed as the day of the Martyrdom of King* Charles I. - - 257

### SERMON

*Preached before the Incorporated Society for the Propagation of the Gospel in Foreign Parts, at their anniversary meeting in the parish church of St.* Mary-le-Bow, *on* Friday February 19, 1773, 295

### SERMON

*Preached in the parish church of* Christ-Church, London, *on* Thursday, April 24, 1777; *being the time of the yearly meeting of the children educated in the charity schools in and about the cities of* London *and* Westminster, 331

# A CHARGE

DELIVERED BY THE

Right Rev. JONATHAN SHIPLEY, D.D.
Lord Bishop of St. Asaph,

To the Clergy of his Diocese, at his Primary Visitation in the Year 1770.

---

HAVING been promoted without any solicitation, and very little desert of mine, to a rank in the Church which requires more wisdom and prudence, and more authority than I have the vanity to assume; I think it my peculiar good fortune to be placed over a body of clergy whose decent manners and exemplary behaviour

## CHARGE I.

haviour will render, if I may credit general report, government an eafy tafk, and fpare me the unpleafant neceffity of employing cenfures and feverity.

As this ftate of things is moft agreeable to my own temper and wifhes, I will indulge the pleafure of believing it, and have the fatisfaction to be confirmed in my opinion by the little experience I have already had myfelf, and the concurrent teftimony of thofe who have been beft acquainted with the ftate of this Diocefe. And though perhaps it may be needlefs to far the greateft part of you, to give inftructions which your whole conduct has fhewn you to be well informed of, yet in matters of very great importance, admonitions of the plaineft kind may be of ufe, even to the wifeft; for all that we know is not always prefent to our minds. I fhall therefore take leave to lay before you,
and

and for my own use as well as yours, a short view of the duties required of us by the virtuous and honourable profession into which we have entered. The province you have undertaken is to instruct your parishes in the rule of duty; of self-government, of their behaviour towards one another, as far as justice and charity are concerned, of the reverence and the obedience that is due to the Author of our Being and of the Universe, and of the fittest methods of expressing it. Now that this is not a contemptible nor useless undertaking, is evident from hence; that in all wise and civilized nations, there has constantly been some establishment to instruct the people in those ceremonies and rules of life, in which, according to their notions, religion and virtue were supposed to consist. And the excellent writings that are left to us on moral subjects, form a proof from the concurrent opinion of the wifest and beft of men in different ages, that inftructions of this fort are of fingular fervice to mankind. But in all thefe inftructions and ceremonies there were great and palpable defects, apparent even to thofe who obferved them. Our Saviour, in the promulgation of the Gofpel, has gracioufly fupplied thofe wants which reafon had pointed out before, and had endeavoured without much fuccefs to relieve.

The Bible, in which thefe comfortable truths are delivered to us, is that good treafure, that ample ftorehoufe, from whence may eafily be drawn thofe ufeful precepts and that valuable knowledge, which are fully fufficient to anfwer all religious and moral purpofes, and to direct the actions of every order of men. He that is beft acquainted with thefe fountains of living waters, will beft be able to collect

collect and difpenfe them in fuch due proportions, as his own wants, and the truft committed to his care may require. The facred doctrines which it is chiefly incumbent upon us to teach, are thofe which our hearers ought not to be ignorant of, and from which they will receive the greateft benefit. The awful truths relating to the divine nature, as far as God has vouchfafed to unfold them to us; the fallen ftate of man, which feems to have been confirmed by the concurrent teftimony of antient tradition, and which is fo fuitable to the experience of our own weaknefs and infirmities; the doctrine of our redemption which nature has fo much caufe to rejoice in, and is fo little able to comprehend, and the almoft apparent neceffity of the manifeftation of God in the flefh to deftroy the works of the devil; thefe are the foundations, the chief corner-ftones of our faith and duty, and ought always to be inculcated with zeal, and heard with reverence. But the chief effect which Scripture teaches us to expect even from these doctrines is upon the lives of men; that, denying ungodliness and worldly lusts, they should live soberly, righteously, and godlily in this present world. It is therefore our business to inforce in the strongest manner the great principles of moral duty, which are held forth to us in Scripture with the most instructive clearness, and in many different lights. Sometimes our duty is represented as a legal tribute paid to the great Creator and sole Proprietor of the Universe; and sometimes as the just return of love and gratitude to our heavenly Father, the giver of all good things, whose tender mercies are over all his works.

In one place our duty to our fellow creatures is put upon a footing of strict justice

justice and equity, and we are commanded to do unto other men as we would they should do unto us. In another place we are instructed to consider all the sons of men as children of one common parent, to love them as ourselves, and to follow that which is good for all men.

These several foundations of our duty should be laid open and explained, and your hearers should be instructed, which is not a difficult task, how easily these principles may be applied to the common occurrences of life, and the situations in which they find themselves placed. In the town and in the country very different duties are required from men, and they are exposed to very different temptations. Now it will be of singular service to caution your hearers against the vices with which they are most easily beset, against that species of intemperance and dishonesty into which their way of life, or the example of their neighbours is most likely to lead them; and much good may be done by putting them in mind of those instances of kindness and right behaviour which they have not been used to practise; for men often continue to be not so good as they themselves would chuse to be, through inattention, and for want of being made sensible of the advantages and propriety of a different behaviour. It might seem needless to mention, if one did not sometimes meet with instances that shew the necessity of it, that whatever instructions you give, they should be couched in plain, intelligible, and familiar language, otherwise they are in reality no instructions at all. And it is difficult to imagine how very necessary it is to observe this rule, if you choose to be understood by the lowest rank of your hearers. Give me leave to

recommend

recommend to you upon this occasion, as an excellent system of religious knowledge, delivered in plain, proper, and significant language, and a model worthy your imitation, the catechetical lectures of our late worthy Metropolitan. But these admonitions, and almost every other I can undertake to give, will be rendered in a manner useless, if you exercise your holy function under a due sense of its importance, and with the zeal and anxiety which a good man must necessarily feel for the success of so excellent a work. Love is of an inventive nature; and the good-will and affection we ought to bear to our flocks will suggest many methods of teaching, and enable you to influence their conduct, and advance their interests more effectually than any cold and formal rules that can be given. For, indeed, your labours will neither be easy to yourselves, nor of much

advantage

advantage to your hearers, unless they are the labours of love. And sure there is no employment which can possibly administer more satisfaction to a reasonable mind, than that of serving and improving our fellow-creatures. The intention itself is virtuous; and pleasure and happiness accompany the exercise of it. Let us not suffer so noble an office, which ought to call forth every thing that is great and amiable in the human mind, to dwindle, through carelessness and indifference, into a mere *opus operatum*.

But after having satisfied all the important services that your duty requires of you, there still will remain, especially in country parishes, a considerable portion of time to be employed in such a manner as shall appear most reasonable to yourselves. Now the serious turn which your profession necessarily inspires into a good mind,
will

will not suffer your hours of leisure to been tirely loft, nor even your amusements, to be totally idle and useless. Such of you as have not too long neglected the learned languages, would do well to continue and improve your acquaintance with the great authors of antiquity; in some of which you will find most faithful and pleasing descriptions of the beauties of nature, in others, judicious and lively records of historical events, moral and prudential rules of conduct, but chiefly pictures of life, characters and manners, given in such feeling words, with such pure propriety of language, and tinctured with such clear good sense as you cannot possibly read and understand, without a sensible improvement. And besides the improvement you cannot help deriving from such exalted wisdom and genius, by studying the originals in the same language, you will often

per-

perceive the force of singular expressions, and understand the customs and allusions you meet with in the sacred writings, more perfectly than any commentaries can teach you: and to the same languages you must have recourse, if you chuse to make yourselves acquainted with the imperfect but valuable remains of ecclesiastical antiquity. But, indeed, I would not dissuade you from applying to any branch of science that suits your taste. Nothing of this kind is without its use, and the pleasure that is felt, and the quick progress that is made, where the subject itself is agreeable, may compensate for the lesser importance of the subject itself.

One part of knowledge however there is, so extensive in the contemplation of it, so useful in the application, with a variety fitted to all tastes, and such degrees of plainness and obscurity as may give suitable

able exercife to all capacities, that I cannot help recommending it to your confideration. It is that kind of Hiftory and Philofophy which is called Natural. The views of the great parts of nature, the beauty of their conftruction, and the variety of ufes for which they are evidently intended, and to which they are admirably adapted, are the very paths of contemplation which lead us moft directly to the knowledge of the great Creator, and which form the mind to that ferious and religious turn of thought which is peculiarly fuitable to your function. And the curious particulars into which every branch of this knowledge refolves itfelf, the endlefs difcoveries which arife from enquiry, or from eafy and obvious experiments, and the ufeful applications of it to the advantages of fociety, and the improvement of arts, in particular that of agriculture, the

moft

most valuable of all, are circumstances that ought to excite the curiosity of those who seek only for entertainment, and the industry of those who wish to be serviceable to their countrymen. Let me remind you, it is chiefly by a diligent and successful prosecution of this kind of knowledge, that this kingdom has acquired its high reputation for genius and science, and the whole nation has profited of the lights derived from hence to the advancement of husbandry, of manufactures and commerce. Permit me, for this reason, and for the sake of the people committed to your care, to wish that you would recommend and encourage the learning of the English language; not that I would wish to abolish the use of your own original and venerable tongue. On the contrary, it deserves to last for ages, as a monument of the antiquity of your nation,

and

and the invincible bravery of your ancestors. But I wish, most sincerely, that the inhabitants of this great Principality, especially those of this diocese, may enjoy every advantage and convenience of life, every improvement in arts, in knowledge, and commerce, in as full measure and extent as the most flourishing part of this island. Let every avenue of knowledge and information be open to them; let them make use of all their natural advantages; let them carry on the improvements in cultivation, which they have so happily begun, and let them learn to manufacture the many excellent productions that abound on the surface, and in the entrails of the soil. And if, by those suggestions which may naturally be expected to arise from your superior knowledge and education, their eyes may be opened, or their industry quickened, to

any

any of these useful works, you will enjoy the purest of all pleasures, in the consciousness of having served your country; you will receive your own share of the public advantage; and you will procure that respect and dignity which is the effect of superior wisdom, and is the best support of your ministerial character. Now, the shortest and readiest way of obtaining such advantages as these, is to adopt the improvements, and imitate the skill and industry, of your neighbours. Abolish all useless and unfriendly distinctions, consider all the inhabitants of the island as natives of the same happy country, as subjects of the same gracious Prince; and as fellow-members of the wisest, the most improved, and the best constituted civil society upon earth. Resemble and copy them, where the resemblance would be to your advantage. Preserve only to yourselves

selves and your countrymen, those honourable and virtuous distinctions which have long been a part of your character. Let them retain their old integrity and courage, their hospitality, their friendly dispositions, and their warm benevolence of heart. These are qualities which, in all ages, have been mentioned to their honour; and which still endear them to all that have the opportunity of knowing them.

I rely too much upon the good sense of my hearers, to believe they can think the subjects I have mentioned undeserving of their attention, or unworthy of this solemnity. It is the proper office of virtue, and a most important branch of our religious duty, to communicate to other men the conveniences and advantages, and the temporal good things of this life; and the most effectual means of doing this is, by proper instruction, to enable them to procure those advantages for themselves. He that can contrive, by any method, to make his neighbours more industrious, does them the greatest service which they can receive from a fellow-citizen, and if he does it with a religious view, will be entitled to a proportionable reward from the Supreme Judge of merit.

The first and the most essential duty of a Clergyman is, to teach the doctrines of the gospel, and to give an example of godly life. This is of indispensible obligation, and till we see proofs to the contrary, we ought to hope and believe, that it belongs to every one of our brethren. But great and valuable as these duties are, it is hardly credible how much the value of them is enhanced, when they are joined with learning, with prudence, and with a general knowledge of the arts of life, and the characters of men. These are qualities

which

which will render your labours pleasant to your hearers and yourselves; which will enable you to give to virtue its most engaging ornaments, and make its beauty appear; and thus you will adorn the doctrine of God, our Saviour, in all things.

Having now gone through such a description of your duties as seemed to me suitable to the present occasion, I hope that you will believe that I am not unmindful of the very great and important charge that rests upon myself. I know how unequal I am to the work I have undertaken, and that my best endeavours will always stand in need of your indulgence, and sometimes of your forgiveness. This unaffected sense of my own weakness, will render me desirous, on all proper occasions, to receive your advice and assistance; and you cannot assist me more effectually

fectually, than by a conscientious discharge of the trust reposed in you; and by supporting that character of decency and virtue, which your behaviour has already gained.

And, let me seriously remind you how very unworthy it would be of that character, by giving testimonials with carelessness and indulgence, to introduce immoral and worthless men into your own respectable body. It will depend entirely upon the integrity of your testimony, whether the persons whom I am soon to ordain are such as will be the credit, or the disgrace of the diocese. And I am unwilling to believe that any of you are capable of imposing upon me in a matter of so much consequence, where I cannot guard against the deceit, and must think it my duty to resent it. But I will not sully the pleasure I take in believing all the good that is said

said of you, by entertaining a thought to your disadvantage. On the contrary, it will be a most pleasing task to me, the most grateful exercise of my office, to make myself acquainted with your different merits and talents; and to use the means that are placed in my power to cherish and reward them. At present, I hope you will give me credit for the goodness of my intentions, and make a reasonable allowance for the restraints and difficulties which unavoidably attend a situation like mine. I must not hope to be so happy as to be always able to do the good that I wish; and I may sometimes err for want of right information, or from mistakes in judgment. Some applications may be made to me of so powerful and so obligatory a nature, that to reject them might be deemed want of justice or gratitude. And I should be insensible to the best of all human feelings, if, in the various scenes of a pretty active life, I had not met with a few who had claims upon me from friendship, from mutual services, and an intimate knowledge of their worth. Yet I will take care to preserve myself, as much as in reason I ought, from the influence of these considerations, and not let them interfere with the just rewards of those, who are most acceptable to the natives of this country, and best able to serve them. For I hope that I shall not be numbered with those aspiring men, who are always pressing forward, and never think themselves sufficiently exalted above their brethren. That odious vice of ambition, which is too apt to ruin the good qualities of those whom it raises, never gave any disturbance to my younger days; and it shall not embitter my age. I shall think myself happy should I be able to perform the duties of of an office, of which I have great reason to fear the burthen, with tolerable satisfaction to my own mind; and merit some share in the esteem of the many worthy and respectable men who make up the Clergy of this Diocese.

# CHARGE II.

Delivered in the Year 1774.

---

THE office of the Clergy in general (and a very important and honourable office it is) is to inſtruct mankind in their duty. And this I hope we perform with zeal and integrity, according to the beſt of our abilities, towards the reſpective congregations that are committed to our care. But, when we meet together on theſe ſolemn occaſions, it then becomes a part of our office to think over and explain our own duty; and to inſtruct and exhort one another. This was the plan I had formed to myſelf

myself, when I addressed you in my primary visitation. I then laid open a general view and description of the obligations that are due from us to civil society, and to the Church of Christ, intending, in the future discourses which God shall permit me to hold on these occasions, to trace our duty through its particular branches and divisions; and to lay down the rules that may render our conduct not only pure and undefiled, but useful and void of offence. At present I am forced to wave my former design, in order to lay before you matters of a public nature; which seemed at first to threaten danger and ruin to our excellent establishment.

The spirit of enquiry is a principle of the most extensive use in human affairs, and has been applied with great advantage to religious subjects; but the love of truth itself may sometimes become excessive, and enquiries may be pushed beyond the limits which neither reason nor piety would chuse to transgress. Besides this, prejudice, ambition, malice, and other bad passions may shelter themselves under an affected zeal for the purity of religion.

Some of these causes I think we may, without any breach of charity, presume to have mingled in the repeated attacks which have been carried on for several years successively against the established church. The Dissenters too of many different denominations have applied, not for a fuller enjoyment of their religious liberty than they at present possess, but for a more clear and explicit declaration of their right to it; and for a repeal of the laws that are unfavourable to it. Now this direct attack upon our church from one quarter, and the zeal for doctrines repugnant to our own from many others,

seem

seem to imply a serious call upon us to examine the foundations of that faith we profess; whether we have built on loose and mouldering sand, or, as we trust, on a firm and immoveable rock. In order to pursue this examination I shall not consider the form of our ecclesiastical government, the primitive institution of episcopacy, nor even the doctrines which distinguish us from the Dissenters, and those among ourselves, who have taken offence at the church in which they have been bred. Was I to enter into these disputes, I could only repeat the arguments which have been retailed for ages on every side, and have left each party in possession of their own opinions. I shall take a different method, which perhaps will not be more satisfactory to ourselves, but appears to me to be better adapted to convince our enemies. Whatever marks there may

may be of the true religion, one of them undoubtedly is to promote the practice of virtue and universal righteousness. Religion is certainly not the invention and creature of civil policy, for it existed prior to civil government. But, as nature and reason have made it necessary for the governing part of every community, to protect and maintain some publick ministers of religion, it is certainly the interest and the wisdom of the state to chuse such as may be teachers of virtue and good morals to their fellow citizens. This is the point of view which should determine a legislator, who respects only the good of his people, in the choice of his religion. And upon this ground I will take leave to say, that the clergy of the established church can plead more merit towards their country than any other religious order of men that ever existed.

Ever

Ever since the days of the reformation, from the Book of Homilies to the excellent writings of our late Archbishop, there has prevailed a sober rational spirit of enquiry; they have studied and given a just description of moral duties, and they have uniformly pursued the same design, each generation improving upon the last. This is a merit, of which our country has enjoyed the fruits without being sufficiently sensible of it. In order to make this clear, it is necessary to recollect what ignorance, what superstition, and what a corrupt kind of casuistry has prevailed in the countries of the Romish religion. Some of their favourite doctrines, the virtues of pardons and indulgences, the intercession of saints, and, what bad men of all persuasions pin their faith upon, and even the good are too apt to give credit to, the efficacy of the mere *opus operatum*;

these

these and whatever besides have a tendency to lessen the obligations of virtue, by finding out some equivalent for it, or some contrivance to do without it, all these things must necessarily retard the progress men might otherwise make in the study of their duty, by rendering them indifferent about it. Happily for our own church, these corrupt doctrines were exploded from the very beginning, for there appears in her articles a temper and moderation, and a knowledge of the right method of interpreting scripture, which does her great honour, considering the prejudices and the philosophy of that age. There is visible, even in the writings of the first reformers, a vein of good sense and sound morals, which those only are competent judges of who are acquainted with the general progress of improvement since their days. How soon after these did
Hooker

Hooker appear, who wrote of Religion and Government, not only with knowledge and accuracy, but with a large and philosophick reach of thought? He was soon succeeded by numbers of able men who profited by his example, who not only defended and explained the religion, but improved the science of their countrymen, and taught them to think and reason. Such was Hales of Eaton, an early pattern of solid learning and candor; who joined great depth of thought with great simplicity of style. Such was the wise and moderate Bishop Taylor; whose 'Liberty of Prophecying' was the first complete piece of good reasoning that England, or perhaps Europe, had seen; in which the rights of conscience and the power of the civil magistrate, are described and taught with as much weight of argument as by any of the great men who came after him,

him, and with a spirit of Christian benevolence superior to any. Contemporary with these was the immortal Chillingworth, whose work has hitherto remained an acknowledged standard of just reasoning, and the most able defence of the Protestant cause. A little prior to him in years was the judicious Bishop Sanderson, who first introduced a more solid and rational manner of preaching, and set an example which was afterwards so much improved upon, by the great men who appeared after the restoration. Then came Barrow; whose comprehensive mind, whose boundless knowledge and commanding flow of eloquence, have made him regarded as one of our most shining lights. He was equalled, though in a different way, by the mild, persuasive, and pathetick Archbishop Tillotson, whose clear interpretation of scripture, whose knowledge of morals, and his skill in adapting the rules of duty to the manners of men and the situations of life, added to a pure, simple, and elegant style, have made him considered ever since, as the most perfect model of Christian instruction. It was in this age that the true philosophy and the rational study of nature first made its appearance; and I cannot help owning that I think it an honour to our Church, that some of the most eminent of our own Clergy were principally concerned, in the institution of that society which has enlightened all Europe; and added so much glory to the British name.

It would be endless for me to describe all the able ministers of the gospel in our own Church, who have flourished since the days of these illustrious men: we may say of them, in general, that they have shown themselves, at first, very able defenders

fenders of their country against popery and arbitrary power; and that, in latter times, they have defended the common cause of religion with great learning and judgment; and the most solid reasoning against the various and perpetual attacks that have been made upon us from the different quarters of infidelity; sometimes open and serious; sometimes concealed under a veil of irony and ridicule, sometimes pretending a great regard for virtue and morals; and sometimes secretly undermining them, or openly disavowing them. But the most remarkable part of their character, has been to have shown a greater attention than any other church, to the practical duties of our religion.

If you look into the writers of the Romish Church, you meet either with loose and dishonest maxims, or with unintelligible raptures and mystery. If you turn to the writers of the Reformed Churches in general; you will meet with much declamation, very superficial reasoning, and great ignorance of the ground of moral duty. The writers of the Dissenters in our own country, till within the last forty years, are so full of the doctrine of salvation by faith alone, and chuse to dwell so little on the necessity of good works, that it would be too much to expect from them, clear and accurate descriptions of moral obligations. But, from the beginning, the Clergy of the Established Church, having been happily free from the speculative opinions which lessen the importance, and discourage the study of our duty, have given a serious and rational attention to the various relations of human life, and the obligations resulting from them. I will venture to say that all Europe cannot produce so many reasonable

treatises

treatises of useful practical religion, written before the end of the last century, as are to be found in our own Church. Add to this, that no order of men have studied the Scriptures with so much judgment and critical skill, by which they have gradually improved the understandings of the people, and have cleared, explained, and, in some instances, have even reformed the doctrines of the Church itself. They have also employed themselves very successfully in the cultivation of science and literature. They have borne a part in the great philosophical discoveries which have done so much honour to our country. They have had almost the entire merit of educating the youth of this kingdom, not only as tutors and governors of the universities, but as teachers of schools, and private instructors in considerable families. And being dispersed in their several parishes over the whole kingdom, we may prefume, without vanity, that to their fuperior knowledge, and their fociety, have been owing, in a great meafure, the general improvement of the people; and that character of good fenfe and ufeful judgment by which they are diftinguifhed from other nations. And, I think, allowing thefe confiderations no more than their due weight, I may take leave to conclude, that the Clergy of the Eftablifhed Church have not been a ufelefs burthen to their country. I may even venture to affirm, that the fingular advantages this nation has reaped from her fkill in commerce, in manufactures, and the mechanical arts, have been owing in a good meafure to that fuperior education, which not only the nobility and gentry, but the middling ranks of life, have derived from the too much undervalued and neglected body of the Clergy. Were we to to enter into a calculation, merely on a temporal view, I doubt not but it would appear that the civil advantages that have redounded to society through our means, have been an ample compensation to our country, for the legal provision she has made for us.

This is a consideration which I think administers great comfort and satisfaction to an honest mind; and, at the same time, ought to be a strong motive with us to continue our improvement in every valuable kind of knowledge that may make us useful to our neighbours. Considered in this light, the credit and dignity of our Church stands upon a solid foundation, as a society that has thought it an essential part of religion to cultivate and teach the purest morals, and many of whose members, by their studious and contemplative lives, have enlarged the boundaries of science, and improved the underſtanding of their fellow citizens. Men of integrity and virtue ought to be very cautious of engaging in any meaſures that may tend to prejudice and undermine, and much leſs to deſtroy a Church that has deſerved ſo well of our country. The virtues ſhe has taught and practiſed, and encouraged, afford a ſtrong preſumption in favour of the truth of her doctrines. But then will they ſay, can ſhe oblige us to ſubſcribe Articles that we cannot believe? By no means. Every man muſt judge for himſelf, and be governed by the dictates of his own conſcience. But then every church muſt have certain rules and principles which are to be conſidered as the terms of communion; otherwiſe her members could not join in the ſame worſhip, or meet together to hear ſuch doctrines as they approve of. The principles that are

agreed

## CHARGE II. 41

agreed upon, and the rules that are laid down, cannot be confidered, even by the church that adopts them, as of equal authority with the Holy Scriptures. It is enough if it can be maintained that they are not inconfiftent with them. Every fet of religious doctrines that are drawn up by man, will certainly partake, in fome degree, of human infirmity, and can hardly efcape being difcoloured by the prejudices, and even by the philofophy of the age. For the fame reafon, fince all human opinions are fubject to frequent changes, it is highly probable that the religious doctrines which fuit one age, will not be fo well received in another. I mean the fpeculative points of which men think fo differently. Upon this account, it ought to be the object of fuch as are employed in drawing up articles of religion, to confine themfelves as much as poffible to what is

clear

clear and fundamental, and to leave as great a latitude in the interpretation of their own laws, as is confiftent with peace and uniformity of worfhip. And it is amazing how well thefe rules were obferved by the compilers of our Articles, confidering the ftate of learning and religious knowledge in the times they lived.

But from hence arifes a queftion, Whether the Articles of Religion muft be perpetually changing with the fluctuating opinions of men? To which we anfwer, that the fame difficulty occurs in all other human laws. The manners and relations of men, and the fituation of things are perpetually changing; and yet the bufinefs of the world is carried on in the moft material points, for a long courfe of years, by the fame laws. The truth is, that it is not neceffary to bring all human actions to one

one common standard. It is every man's duty to search after truth, but it is not necessary, because it is not practicable, that all men should believe precisely the same set of truths: and, doubtless, it would be the true wisdom of every church, at proper intervals, to revise her own Articles. That would remove the doubts and difficulties of tender consciences, and let them know exactly what it is expected they should believe. At present, it appears that our ablest divines have gradually departed from some rigorous interpretations of the Articles that prevailed at first: this is not unknown to those who alone have authority to determine what is most expedient for us; and we doubt not, but in their own good time, they will consent to have the burdens that are complained of, removed. In the mean while, it is our duty to apply, with a godly sincerity,

the

the learning and talents we are feverally bleffed with, to the fincere and accurate ftudy of the Holy Scriptures, to which the compilers of our Articles appeal for the truth of what they teach, and which, we truft would lead unprejudiced minds to that excellent Church, of which we profefs ourfelves to be members. And let us remember that we can no way do her more effectual fervice, than by cultivating that fuperiority of learning and knowledge, which has hitherto been fo honourable to the Clergy, and fo ufeful to the Public.

I fhould have taken no notice of the Petition of the Diffenters, if it had not been confidered, I think unjuftly, as an attack upon the Church. There feems to be no reafon on our fide for refufing them a legal title to that liberty of confcience which we have fo long permitted them to enjoy

enjoy without any public inconvenience. In general, it muſt be owned, they anſwer the character they have acquired of good citizens, and decent, induſtrious men; and their teachers, of late years, by many uſeful works of learning and ſcience, and particularly by many judicious explications of the moral and practical parts of duty, have ſet us an example of diligence and application, in which it would not be for our credit to be outdone. And, if ſome of them have erred from the faith in thoſe doctrines to which we juſtly aſcribe peculiar ſanctity, and more of them have been ſuſpected (we hope unjuſtly) of doing ſo, ſtill it becomes more obligatory upon us to inform ourſelves of eccleſiaſtical hiſtory, and of all the ſubtleties and wiles of diſputation, that we may be able to eſcape and confute them, and to vindicate and eſtabliſh that plain ſenſe of Scripture

which

which the whole tenor of revelation points out to us, but the pride of learning is not always willing to submit to.

In general there appears to be most strong and peculiar obligations upon our Order, to labour, with great perseverance, to improve ourselves in all the branches of divine and human knowledge, particularly in such as are more immediately useful to society. This is evidently necessary in order to support that high character of knowledge and wisdom which our Church has hitherto sustained. And much more is required, at present, to preserve our names from contempt; and to keep alive those useful impressions of respect and dignity, which contribute so much to the success of our labours, much more, I say, is required at present, when knowledge is become more general; and men may justly be offended, if the Order that is maintained

tained to instruct the rest, shall not appear to be more knowing and more virtuous than their neighbours.

I thought to have ended here; but in the present state of things, perhaps, it may not be unsuitable to the character I sustain, to caution you against suffering yourselves to be infected with the spirit of riot and licentiousness, which is spread through great part of your congregations. There is nothing blameable in showing your regard in a serious, a decent, and even a zealous manner, for the person or the cause that you approve. It were to be wished, indeed, that men would employ more care and discernment than they frequently do, in the choice of representatives, on whose integrity the publick welfare depends.

But to take an active and a noisy part in the conduct of elections; to submit to low

low offices and disgraceful familiarities; to hope to gain favour and rise to preferment by practices unsuitable to the character of a clergyman, has something in it peculiarly shocking and offensive to a serious mind, and makes even those who are forced to employ such persons ashamed to reward them. I mention not this by way of reproof, for I can say with pleasure, that I know of none that deserve it. On the contrary, I know of many under my care, whose learning and goodness are recommended by a modest and prudent behaviour, that gains them the respect of their neighbours and the friendship of their superiors. Such characters it shall be my business to find out and to reward. I can say with pleasure, that I know no diocese in this kingdom, where the clergy in general are more decent, more virtuous, and more respectable; and I believe there

## CHARGE II.

is no diocese in which they are so much respected Instances 'of immoral and scandalous behaviour are very rare, and they ought to be rare indeed. It is our business to improve and cultivate whatever we may have that is useful and praiseworthy; and to supply, as well as we can, the defects that all of us are liable to. As for me, it will be the fault of my judgment, and not of my intention, if I do not dispose of the rewards which Providence has committed to my distribution, so as to answer the purposes of public good. Uncommon virtue, joined with uncommon learning, ought to have a claim superior to every other recommendation, and my own heart would condemn me, if I did not listen to it. Indeed, I have felt more true happiness in serving a worthy man, unasked, than in complying with all the solicitations of the Great. Assure yourselves

selves that I sincerely wish and endeavour to promote the welfare of my clergy and my diocese, and allow me to hope, that your candour and indulgence will excuse my failings.

# TO THE READER.

THE doctrine contained in the following Charges, is neither new, nor obscure; and was evidently such as the times called for. Yet, as it may be thought, by some, unsuitable to those assemblies in which it was delivered, I shall take leave to say a few words in explanation. And here I would observe, that although it may be justly considered as the distinguishing honor of the church of England, that she has taught the moral duties with more clearness, and in a more reasonable manner, than any other Christian community, yet one species of duty there is, which all sects and professions have almost equally neglected to teach, I

mean

mean the duties of public men, and the duties which all of us owe to our country. But be this as it may, I am bold to assert, that the teachers of a religion whose principle is to do good to all men, cannot, without deserting their office, forbear to teach the duties of princes and magistrates, and to shew the guilt and ruin arising from the violation of those duties. On such occasions it becomes necessary to raise our conceptions above the common business of private life, and venture to apply the simple precepts of our Saviour to the greatest and most important operations of government. In the plainness of those precepts there is a depth and wisdom that are sufficient to direct the highest actions of men: it is here, as in the most perfect systems of philosophy, where the simplest laws are employed to direct the most complicated motions, and the most immense forces.

forces. Nor is it surprising to find such resemblance in the workmanship of the same God. Tell us not, then, that religion is merely a transaction between God and the soul—it is the language of hypocrites and enthusiasts, or of obscure and useless men. The religion of a Christian, in public employment, should be as evident as the virtue of a Phocion or an Aristides, and in common cases exert itself in the same manner.

Those heroes were led by the light of nature, and the importance of objects, to consider the service of their country as the first of human duties, which we seem to have rejected from our religion as a useless and perished branch. For how few are there now, who consider the service of the public in any other light than as the means of making a fortune! perhaps it may be said, and with some degree of plaufibility, that religion has nothing to do with politics, but then it may be faid with equal propriety, that merchandize or hufbandry have no concern with religion; and yet religion is allowed to govern the actions of the merchant and the farmer, and furely it is of as much importance that it fhould govern the conduct of the ftatefman.

Religion has certainly nothing in its nature contrary to government. The misfortune is, we attempt to excufe every thing in public life, by calling it politics. The rules of our duty feem not to extend to public tranfactions. From whence we fee men of decent and almoft virtuous characters, do things which in private tranfactions their fouls would abhor.

Let them, however, be reminded, that the fublimity of the Chriftian morals, confifts in the ufefulnefs, the extent, the
univerfality

universality of the principles; that they give laws not only to the vulgar, but to statesmen, princes, and law-givers themselves.

The duties of government are undoubtedly the most important of all to society; and the transgression of them is the highest guilt that is in the power of mankind to incur. Look into the historical part of the Old Testament, and you will see the unerring Spirit of God reproving injustice and oppression, with a language and freedom, that very much resemble the indignation which such crimes have always raised in virtuous and generous minds. But the benevolent spirit of Christianity furnishes a still stronger argument against arbitrary power. its whole doctrines breath the most liberal, public, and universal friendship. That law which requires us to love all men, will certainly not permit us to neglect or abuse those with whom we are most intimately connected, and to whom we are most obliged

I do not say that the ministers of religion should censure in public the measures of this, or that, Administraion, but I do say that they should consider themselves as the teachers of whatever is good and useful to mankind, or in other words, as teachers of the gospel. And sure it becomes a bishop, who is himself a member of the legislature, to mark the crimes and the customs that religion condemns. Nay, I am bold to affirm, the noblest office a bishop can be employed in, is to teach the great duties of magistrates; the law of universal kindness, and the particular obligations that princes are under, not to corrupt the manners of the people committed to their charge.

Let the clergy, like 'the rest of their
fellow

fellow subjects, pay all due submission to the powers that are set over us for our good, tribute to whom tribute, honor to whom honor is due. But let them teach the greatest their duty; that they are not only servants of our common master, but, by the very tenure of their office, servants of the people. Let them always recommend in the most powerful manner the virtues of disinterestedness, of humanity, of public spirit to our rulers; since on their good conduct depend not only the wealth and happiness of us subjects; but we are such frail creatures that even our good principles, the purity of our religion, the knowledge of our rights, our talents and our virtues, depend upon the generous or oppressive treatment we meet with from those who govern us.

Under such impressions Dr. Shipley, then

then bishop of St. Asaph, addressed his clergy in the years 1778, and 1782.

At the former period we had begun to feel severely the effects of our fatal contest with America, and the latter was the commencement of the Rockingham administration, which, however discordant in its parts, undoubtedly contained as much virtue, and as great abilities, as this or any country could produce.

The Right Rev. Prelate was forced to judge like his neighbours of the characters of men by their actions: yet he has most studiously avoided personal reflections. He thought it became not, and was indeed beneath a teacher of the gospel, to censure the conduct of individuals; it was his part to point out what they owe to God and their country, and to God and their country he commits their reward or punishment.

## TO THE READER.

punishment. He lived to see the times change; and our calamities advance upon us with a rapidity that rendered the sentiments that were suitable to those years, a very imperfect representation of the more melancholy years that followed. He lived to see a peace as humiliating and disgraceful as our enemies could wish; and yet, in our situation, perhaps as good as could be made. He lived to see the experience, the merit, and the reputation of good and wise men no proof against the temptations that government can offer.

He saw all friendship dissolved; and that generous band who held so long together, broken and separated, or connected with others the most unlike themselves. But he did not live to see his country rising superior to such accumulated misfortunes, and restored to a degree of splendor, consequence, and prosperity, which in those

those days the most sanguine durst not have anticipated.

At a time like the present, when those strong features which formerly distinguished Whigs from Tories, are in a great measure lost, when many who are Whigs in theory are downright Tories in practice, it may be proper to observe, that there is such a thing as the character of an honest man distinct from that of Whig or Tory. And this distinction consists, according to my humble idea, in acting, as far as the times will admit, with men of principle and honor, and not in following even them, when they act in opposition to the public good.

Such, I am proud to say, was the very honorable and very unprofitable line of conduct which the Bishop of St Asaph uniformly pursued. It was this which drew him from the quiet, unpretending station of private life, which led him to quit

quit the beaten track of preferment; to refuse offers which have seldom fallen to the lot of his profession; and to follow where justice, duty, and the interest of the public called him.

At the beginning of the American war, he saw the consequences of that unwise and pernicious measure; the effects of which, from the enormous debt contracted by it, our country must feel for ages. He took at once a decided part, he ventured to differ from his friends, and even from the respectable minister who had raised him: and joined a set of men to whom he was a perfect stranger, but who appeared to him to understand, and pursue the true interests of their country. He soon acquired an intimacy with the heads of the party, and those who survive, will do him the justice to acknowledge, he never entered into the passions and jealousies that
prevailed

prevailed amongst them; but for several years persisted in endeavouring to persuade the leaders of that party, that their interest and honor, and the safety of their country, consisted in their union. What were his Lordship's religious sentiments, his works will best declare, from these also it will appear, that his attachment to our happy constitution, in church and state, was zealous and unfeigned. He was a warm and steady friend to the most unlimited toleration. He justly conceived that " no church has a right to impose articles of faith on any other religious community*." and that the magistrate, instead of preventing men from worshiping God in their own way, ought to encourage the worshipping of him in any way, if he means to encourage virtue and piety. He was no less a friend to the civil liberty of mankind;

* Vide Speech on Toleration.

he was ready to admit all sects and professions into a participation of the common rights of their fellow citizens; but with this invariable and decided proviso, that their tenets did not militate against the established government we live under. What would have been *now* his opinion respecting the repeal of the Test and Corporation Acts, may be improper for me to determine. It rests upon the simple question, whether the language *lately* held by those who wish to be considered as holding forth the general opinion of the Dissenters, comes within the above exception.

These are the principles in which Dr. Shipley lived and died, and to those who know how to value such principles, this publication will not be unacceptable.

The PUBLISHER.

# CHARGE III.

Delivered in the Year 1778

---

MY first idea of the method to be observed in the composition of those solemn Charges which it is my duty to give; was to explain as well as I was able, what is the best kind of religious instruction, and what the best means of conveying it, in order to cultivate those useful and domestic virtues, which ensure all the blessings and comforts of private life; and make men happy without wealth or ostentation. I wish to convince our hearers and ourselves, that religion is no austere, melancholy, useless thing; but our best counsellor and guide in the common bufinefs of life; that aims in all fituations to render us as happy as prudence, reafon, and virtue can make us. Once I have been diverted from this grateful employment, by the neceffity of paying fome attention to the difputes, concerning the Articles of our church, and thofe facred rights of confcience which all men are very ready to claim, and too unwilling to grant. At prefent the whole attention of our minds, our beft, and ftrongeft feelings, are all turned towards the melancholy profpect of our public affairs. By a long feries of unfortunate counfels and events, we find every thing that was dear and precious in the eyes of our anceftors, either loft, or brought into the utmoft danger. It is hard, it is painful to the hearts of Britons to give up all our fond ideas of national glory and empire, that vanity of noble minds which we had

perhaps

perhaps too warmly indulged.—The aweful and salutary discipline of Providence is now teaching us an humbler lesson.—But since almost every human misery is owing to some neglect or transgression of our duty, we ought to regard our public misfortunes as a providential call upon us to consider the nature of our public duties. In order to do this in as useful a manner as the shortness of the time will allow, I will suppose you to be already acquainted with the origin and principles of civil government from whence those duties arise. I will suppose you to know, that civil society, like every other species of society, was first instituted for the benefit of those who enter into it; *i. e.* for the benefit of the people. Its first beginnings, like that of all other human contrivances, were weak, simple, and imperfect; small numbers met together in little districts, perhaps like our parishes; either to assist each other in guarding against some general danger, or in performing some works in common; from whence every one was to derive an advantage. The benefits they afterwards experienced which were not foreseen; and the pleasures and comforts arising from the habits and use of society, drew many more into the union, and formed by degrees the rudiments of a commonwealth. But every step they took, every regulation they invented, every magistrate they chose, was evidently with a view to preserve peace and security, and to attain happiness. It is a pleasant, a liberal, and useful speculation, and which I would venture to recommend to such as feel themselves capable of pursuing it, to observe the progress, the changes, and the various forms of government, with the different degrees of happiness or misery attending them, as they may

may be collected from the records of hiſtory, joined to our own experience and obſervation. Government is certainly a moſt important portion of the buſineſs of mankind; and it is alſo, perhaps, the moſt valuable branch of natural philoſophy: but that purſuit would far exceed the bounds of our preſent enquiry.

The origin of government was certainly meant for the good of thoſe civil ſocieties which firſt made uſe of it. The powers granted to the firſt magiſtrates were few and ſimple; and they were given only for the preſent occaſion. In the earlieſt and moſt authentic of all hiſtories, it appears that the Iſraelites were governed at firſt by judges, a temporary magiſtracy, and of very limited powers. It was only great and ſignal occaſions that prompted them to ſeek for ſome one to go before them to battle. In the moſt remote ages of antiquity,

quity we find there is as little appearance of art and contrivance in their governments as in their manners. The increase of wealth, and the improvements of life, introducing numberless new interests and competitions, the art of governing great bodies of men became a very complicated work, of much contrivance and labour. But, unfortunately, it grew necessary to enlarge the powers of government, before experience had taught men the danger of enlarging them too much. If we want to know by what a number of progressive steps that vast machine has been brought to its present form, we may recollect what kind of little states and principalities are described as established in Greece, by the earliest historians and poets; or in our own country, in the obscure annals of our first ancestors. Such, indeed, are still to be found, in the tribes of Indians in the eastern ein and western parts of the world: consider through what a long series of experiments, what numberless revolutions, what dreadful changes between anarchy and despotism, the race of men must have passed, in their progress from that early period, to the present unwieldy form of society.

In the governments of Europe at this day, we see the effects of time, industry, and experience, working slowly for ages on human nature. The migrations and mixtures of nations, the inventions of arts, the improvements of navigation, and the progress of commerce, together with the influence of religion, of habit, of national character, and all those unknown causes that act perpetually upon our minds and bodies, which we call by the names of Chance and Accident, all these have concurred with the talents and characters of extraordinary men, to introduce new ranks and orders of society; to point out the propriety of different offices and regulations, and to form the present system of manners, customs, and laws, which we call Government.

I have endeavoured to express myself more fully upon this subject, for the sake of introducing an observation that appears to me of very great importance; it is this; that the gradual and progressive manner in which governments were formed, is an indisputable proof that society may subsist, and actually has subsisted, for ages, without lodging an absolute and unlimited sovereignty in any particular hands. I will add further, that ever since insatiable lust of power and dominion has exercised the hearts of ambitious men, it has never yet, in one single instance, attained that full arbitrary sway it is condemned to long for in vain. Those who trample upon the laws

and

and rights of a people, are yet forced to refpect their opinions, their prejudices, and even their follies. The very inftruments of their power become checks and bars to the exercife of it, and fometimes become the inftruments of its deftruction. Providence, in mercy to mankind, has fet bounds, in the nature of things, which wicked men cannot overpafs. Within thofe limits, government is the work of human invention. Its laws and powers have been formed and regulated, not by the abftract ideas of fpeculative men, who, of all men are the moft ignorant of human affairs, but by the opinions and bufinefs of the world, and chiefly from the ignorance and negligence with which the people defend their rights, and the art and violence with which bad men attack them. Perhaps there is no government at prefent exifting, which owes not fome part of its conftitution conſtitution to fraud and uſurpation. But whatever prejudice, in length of time, the liberties of men may have ſuffered from the ambition of their fellow-citizens; government, at its origin, was certainly intended for the good of the ſeveral ſocieties which firſt made uſe of it. Men had not then acquired thoſe ideas of unlimited ſovereignty which have grown up in after ages; from the incroachments of princes, the tameneſs of the people, the flattery of courtiers, and the ſophiſtry of divines and lawyers. That was the work of after times; and of long habits of fear, ſervility, and adulation. By degrees, men ſeemed to have loſt ſight of their own original intentions, and their governors have often had the confidence, from the ſucceſs of their uſurpations, to conſider their own will and pleaſure as the end of their office: to conſider themſelves not as the truſtees of a people,

people, but as the owners of a flock; as the lords of subjects, whose only duty is to submit.

I will not attempt to explain on how just a title these pretensions were founded; that you will find discussed, in the most ample and satisfactory manner, in the writings of Mr. Locke, and of my venerable friend and patron the late Bishop Hoadley. Only let me observe to you, that these different ways of thinking we have mentioned, one of which considers princes as the trustees, and the other as the proprietors, of their people; have produced two very different inferences concerning the powers and the prerogatives of civil government.

Those who think government instituted for the sole use and emolument of the persons who govern, must necessarily think their powers unlimited. For, on this supposition, their interests alone are to be regarded,

garded, of which they are the only judges; and who will set bounds to their own pretensions? But they who believe government to be instituted purely for the good of the governed; will naturally suppose that the powers of their rulers are, in all cases, to be limited by the end for which those rulers were appointed. And, as they must have observed that the other opinion has, in all countries, very numerous and very formidable supporters, and in practice, at least, has prevailed almost universally; they must regard it as a chief point of civil wisdom to trust no more power to princes than is strictly necessary to procure the good of society. Nor should this be considered as a disadvantage even by the prince himself, for the happiest state that man can be placed in, is, to be endowed with great powers of doing good, and, at the same time, to be preserved from the temptation

tation to do evil, from the dangers of an unbounded trust, and from the pride and intoxication of arbitrary power. God, who knoweth the weakness of the sons of men, for their own sakes, has rendered every one of them dependant and accountable. Unlimited sovereignty belongs only to him who is qualified to exercise it, by unlimited wisdom and unlimited benevolence. But very little of this kind of reasoning is necessary to convey to our hearers that degree of knowledge concerning government, which will answer all the ends of edification. In this, as in all other cases, it is sufficient for us to recur to that law which God has revealed to us for the direction of our lives. The principles of the gospel will instruct princes to observe a right course of action, and, at the same time, will enable us to judge of their conduct.

Our

Our great lawgiver was himself present, and instrumental in the creation of this immense world, every thing in that original plan of the universe, was ordered by weight and measure, for divine wisdom was present at the council. Innumerable orders of beings were formed, and innumerable worlds were prepared for their reception. The instincts and faculties with which every species was endued, the situations in which they were placed, the apartments and accommodations that were provided for them, and the companions with whom they were appointed to live, were fully sufficient to teach all beings the law of their nature, by pointing out the means of their preservation and happiness. This instruction is given by nature to the beasts of the field and the fowls of the air. But to us God has given reason and judgment, and left it to ourselves, from our circumstances,

stances, our wants, and our relations, to collect the will of our Creator, and our own duty. And left our weakness and prejudices should sometimes betray us into wrong conclusions; our Lord, as the last finishing of his divine work, has graciously given the clearest revelation of his will in the gospel. Even there, he only discovers to us the great principles and outlines of the law that is to govern us. The application to particular cases is left to exercise our own judgment and discretion: for our all-wife Governor seems to be jealous of the honour which is due to the understanding he has given us. He expects and requires that we should live in the constant exercise of it.

Now, the great object of this universal wisdom is not merely to enforce the inferior and subordinate duties of life, to direct the little charities, and the orderly
devotions

devotions of obscure private men, (though no instance of goodness is so minute as to escape its influence); but to instruct mankind to act a useful and becoming part in the various trying occasions of real life to form good parents, good citizens, and good magistrates; and shew how every office, and every member of society, should contribute to the interest of the whole.

Your memories will easily suggest to you the numberless passages in scripture which breathe this spirit of universal love and benevolence. Now, it is one of the clearest and simplest consequences of such doctrine as this, that the rulers of the people, who are possessed of so large a share of power; whether by grant, or inheritance, or however acquired, are strictly obliged, as Christians, to use it to the benefit of their subjects, who are also their brethren.

Their

Their true pre-eminence confifts in being ftewards of a larger portion of the divine bounty, and their duty in a right diftribution of it. But it has, in all ages, been the employment of flatterers and interefted men, to fet princes free from thefe obligations. Even the minifters of the gofpel themfelves, have been too much inclined to relax the duties which it was a principal part of their office to enforce. The fuggeftions of intereft and difcretion; the impofing airs of grandeur, and the fear of offending thofe who were the mafters of their fortunes; have induced even men of character to foothe the ears of princes with the detail of their rights, their fovereignty, and the obedience due to them; rather than honeftly to exact at their hands thofe public fervices, to fecure the performance of which, their fovereignty and all its rights were given.

We have been told that our Saviour's discourses all related to the actions of private men. If by this is meant, that the actions of princes and rulers are not under the controul of the gospel precepts, there never was yet taught a more pernicious and impious heresy. Are they under weaker obligations than their fellow-citizens to the love of God and their neighbour? Is it not the duty of sovereigns and statesmen, as well as subjects, to be honest men? Can they be good princes and good statesmen without it? It is true the Saviour of the World was no Courtier; he neither wanted the protection, nor sought the society of the Great. His own high office placed him far above all principalities and powers, and the powers and distinctions which men covet so ardently, and usually employ so ill, were of small estimation in his sight; who values us not for our wealth,

wealth, and power, and titles; but for those better qualities of the heart and mind which are precious in the sight of God, which princes cannot give, though they can too often corrupt and destroy. His doctrines are of the most extensive and universal kind; he founds his instructions in righteousness and holiness, in justice and mercy, in the love of God and our neighbour. These principles pervade every period and every station of human life, and are useful and becoming in all. From these great sources he expects that every man, princes as well as others, should draw the rules of their conduct. Let them consult their circumstances, their understandings, and their own hearts, for the application; they will then see that their duties spring from the power they have received, the throne they sit on, and the sceptre they bear. Their office and greatneſs themſelves, are the ſource of their obligations. Their ſovereignty makes them accountable for all the power it gives, and all the benefits it can produce.

But the inſtitution of government is from heaven, and it therefore muſt in no caſe be reſiſted.—Here, if we have the courage to think for ourſelves, we ſhall deny both the aſſertion that is made, and the conſequence that is drawn from it. It does not appear from ſcripture that government is of divine inſtitution, in any other ſenſe than that in which every other ſpecies of ſociety may be derived from the ſame original. All the inſtitutions and inventions of man are ultimately to be referred to God, as their Author. There is certainly nothing divine in the uſual methods of forming, or adminiſtring civil government; all that we ſee of it is purely human, and not always the beſt of the kind.

kind. It is the ordinance of man to which we are juftly bound to fubmit, for the Lord's fake.

But fuppofe, for once, that their commiffion was undoubtedly divine, fuppofe, if you pleafe, that every monarch's acceffion was attefted by figns and wonders, by thunders and lightnings from above, and all that facred terror and amazement with which the voice of God was heard from Mount Sinai;—even then, what elfe could be the effect of this aweful and divine folemnity, but to enforce more ftrongly the obligations to righteoufnefs and mercy; which are the foundations of every lawful throne. In whatever manner the fovereignty is confirmed, the commiffion under which it is held, and the duties refulting from it, are ftill the fame. And, becaufe the obligations impofed are more public,

more solemn, and more personal; it would be the strangest of all conclusions from thence to infer, that, on account of these very circumstances, the sovereign is empowered to break them all with impunity. But, however, true it is that Christian princes do not reign without a divine commission; and fortunately we have the original conveyed to us in the words of our great Lawgiver himself.—" Ye know that
" the princes of the Gentiles exercise do-
" minion over them; and they that are
" great exercise authority over them. but
" it shall not be so with you; for whoso-
" ever will be great among you, let him
" be your servant."

According to this description, the whole duty of a Christian prince consists in being the servant of the public. And there is not a sentiment in the whole Bible more worthy

worthy of God made manifest in the flesh. And lest princes should think the office mean and degrading, the Son of God has ennobled the employment by setting the example. " Even as the Son of Man (for " so the Son of God condescends to call " himself) came not to be ministered unto, " but to minister, and to give his life a ran- " som for many." The conditions annexed to sovereignty are to serve and protect those over whom you reign, to diffuse safety, order, and happiness. These are conditions fit for God to impose upon them whom he advances to the government of their fellow-creatures. They are the conditions which he has prescribed to himself in the government of the world. This, surely, is one of our Saviour's speeches, which relates not only to private men. But, in fact, every sentence of indefinite instruction to be found in the gospel is

directed

directed to all men. The principles of right conduct, in public and private life, are exactly the same. The virtues which are cultivated with the greatest advantage in a private station, have all their functions in public scenes, and even appear with greater use and lustre. Indeed, what in common life is honesty, benevolence, and disinterestedness, acquires dignity in a monarch, and becomes magnanimity, clemency, heroism. The exertions of virtue which are not unusual in inferior characters, appear, from their very rareness, great, sublime, and almost supernatural, in princes. Judge, then, how unfavourable are the highest ranks to the cultivation of real goodness, and the true happiness of man, and learn from hence to respect your own conditions, and to set a just value on the safety, the moderation, the true friendships, the rational improvements, and the
domestic

pleasures that grow up of themselves in the middle path of life.

As for the privilege, which in many nations is supposed to belong to princes, of committing all sorts of violence with impunity; that certainly is not founded on the words of Christ. The high commission under which they act, does not entitle them to violate any single article of it. And if the laws of their country have paid them the compliment not to suppose them capable of being criminal, to turn this generous confidence into a plea for injustice, may itself be justly considered as the greatest of all crimes. God forbid that it should ever more become necessary in this country to deliberate concerning the punishment of princes. May they learn wisdom from the ill success of former usurpations! Other nations who have bowed their neck to the yoke, and have never known a better state,

may

may seek for some degree of ease and quiet in a blind unlimited submission; but with us every right we claim, and every blessing we enjoy, must remind us that every one of them was secured to us by the generous struggles of our ancestors against arbitrary will.

To require passive obedience of Britons, is to require a formal renunciation of all their old habits and principles; of their rights, their liberties, and their senses. If it be asked, what then is the just and true security of a good prince? I answer, the laws of his country, and the love of his people. The art of preventing insurrections and rebellions, is not to take from the people the power to resist, but to make it their interest to obey. Unnumbered monarchs have ruined themselves and their posterity by enlarging their prerogative; but none was ever dethroned

for

for the wisdom and justice of his government. Those are royal virtues that occasion no resistance. Against these there is no law. The nature of man is not changed by the rank he holds: the virtues and talents that were cultivated with advantage in a private station; will have their proper functions in the office of a monarch, and appear with still greater use and lustre. Even patience, humility, and self-denial are not the virtues of subjects only. The very highest stations afford the noblest room for exercising them. They whose actions are of most importance, but subject to the turns of time and chance, have continual occasion for patience: they who are surrounded by flatterers, have constant employment for humility, and wretched are the subjects where the prince denies himself nothing that his power will permit. Righteousness and mercy; or in the

modern

modern use of language, justice, and benevolence, are so far from being fit to be excluded from the cabinets of princes, that good government is nothing else but the full exercise and display of those sovereign virtues. They contain in themselves the very art and mystery of true policy. They are not beneath the attention of the greatest monarchs; since God himself does not disdain to use them in the government of the world. And all the ministerial arts and refinements which lead through the crooked paths of policy, falsely so called; are a sort of unwise cunning, that leads only to guilt and disgrace, and to cheat, and betray the people it was their duty to protect. Let it be allowed me to mention one instance of this false policy with a becoming dread and abhorrence; the art of government by a corrupt influence and bribery. Perhaps human nature does
not

not afford a ftronger inftance of the power of habit to make men do wrong. It is unneceffary, and improper for me to fay, how long this practice has prevailed, and how far it has extended in our own country. There is a decency attending our profeffion that juftly reftrains us from provoking paffions and enmities by perfonal cenfures, but there is alfo a dignity in truth, which ought to embolden us to inform the greateft of their duty. It is the fault of the people in all countries to be credulous and generous, and to place a too unfufpecting confidence in their rulers; from whence it has happened, that in moft nations, except our own, the appearance, or name of freedom is hardly to be met with. But if any thing upon earth is facred, it is the rights which a people have exprefsly referved to themfelves, after trufting every thing elfe to the difcretion of of their rulers. Such, with us, is the security of our perfons; a trial by known laws and unprejudiced judges, and, above all the independency of parliament; especially of your own representatives To undermine thefe rights, and to corrupt thefe reprefentatives; is to deprive us of all that is valuable in our free government, and to ruin the very effence of our conftitution. Under the appearance and the expenfive forms of limited monarchy, it fubjects us, in effect, to arbitrary Will. It mocks men with the image of liberty, while it flips on their fetters, and rivets them faft.

Every man who has a heart to feel, or eyes to fee, muft perceive the injuftice, the ingratitude, the breach of truft, and the pure confummate iniquity of this corrupt influence. Every act of government in fuch circumftances becomes an act of

fraud

fraud and dishonesty; and the evil is not the less, by assuming the appearance of law and liberty. But the worst of all, is, the general profligacy of character, which must necessarily be introduced, by making honors and titles, and offices, the reward of betraying our country. Honesty and integrity are an immediate disqualification for any employment of trust, or profit. Pursue the consequences of this sort of administration in your own minds, and see what at last it must produce. The true end of government is to make men better and happier, the plain and visible end of corruption, is to make then worthless and miserable; and a better expedient for that purpose has never yet been invented. This, at least, I may presume to say is a species of government which is not of divine appointment But perhaps it may be asked, whether I think our own government is arrived at that state of corruption I have been describing? God forbid that I should be able to affirm it. It is not our province to ascertain matter of fact, but to describe the limits of duty.

Mathematicians often assist themselves in the discovery of truth, by supposing cases not only that do not, but that cannot exist. Yet I would ask for no greater blessing than to have the manners and the constitution of this country pure, and incorrupt, I should then think ourselves far safer and happier, notwithstanding the present magnitude of our public misfortunes, than in the career of our old triumphs. I need not at present undertake to shew what duties and public services are indispensably required in all the inferior departments of government. The same chain of obligation runs through all the variable connections of human life. Every

man

man in his place is bound to do what service he can to his fellow creatures, and to employ his best understanding and judgment in the choice of the means.

This appears to be the sovereign law that is given to all human, and perhaps to all intelligent beings. Men, therefore, who have the use of their reason, and a sense of their duty; will judge of the nature and extent of their obligations, by the importance of what they do. They will see, for instance, that it is not quite agreeable to the benevolent spirit of the gospel, to do more mischief by a single vote, than the virtues of the longest private life can atone for. Can they be spectators of the present distresses, and the approaching ruin of their country, and yet think it a matter of total indifference what measures they consent to, and approve of? Let us make every candid allowance for prejudices and habits,

habits; for the connections which it is so natural to follow, and for the influence which it is so difficult to resist. Yet some limits, surely, should be set to the warmth of gratitude and the views of interest. The mere ceremony of voting is an action totally indifferent in itself; and is usually countenanced on both sides of a question by so many considerable characters, that common minds are apt to be satisfied with the authority of their own party, and to disregard the consequences We have read of magic characters, and images, that could inflict tortures and the pangs of death at the greatest distances. We know, for we have seen, that it is possible for the votes of a great council to send fire, slaughter, and desolation to the ends of the earth; and we begin to know that it is possible for these calamities, by a

dreadful

dreadful reverberation, to return ten fold to the country that first caused them.

Now is it possible that men can feel innocent, while they are producing the greatest of all human evils; evils which, after causing the disgrace and torment of their own age and country, may be transmitted to future generations; and last as long as the present constitution of nature? But where, it may be asked, is the mischief of giving a single vote, which makes no change in the public determinations; and perhaps acquits a debt of respect and gratitude, or avoids the resentment of a power which we are not able to contend with? In answer to this, after execrating that infamous perversion of government, which makes it in any case penal to follow the light of evidence, and the dictates of conscience, we need only observe, that the intermixing of these interested considera-

tions in public affairs, is the very principle that forms all the evils we groan under; and makes the cure of them so desperate. Upon this subject men ought to distrust their own integrity. Their selfishness may easily induce them to make very unfair estimates of the mischief they do by their votes. The ruin of a country comprehends such a monstrous, such an enormous aggregate of guilt and misery, that to have contributed to it, only in a small proportion, far exceeds all the crimes which it is possible for a private man to commit. Such arguments as these we have been examining, are the vain suggestions and artifices of dishonest and unhappy minds, that seek for comfort in a soil where it will not grow. But let us not be deceived; guilt is not divisible into shares, nor is it to be lessened by the selfish apologies, or encouraging examples with
which

which men seek to disculpate themselves. He that, with a full knowledge of the subject, gives his assent and support to any pernicious measure; whether those who concur with him are many or few, or whether the design succeeds or miscarries; is himself guilty of the whole. The eye of Divine Justice searcheth the reins, and the heart, and has always the fullest evidence to decide upon. If it be said, that, in supporting the most destructive measures, they still follow the example of many honest and virtuous men; we need only recollect, that if this apology was admitted, there would be a standing justification provided at once for every thing that was profligate and detestable. There are no measures, of the most dangerous tendency, but some good men are found weak enough to approve.

Far be it from me to undervalue the

meanest kind, or the lowest degree, of goodness, wherever it is found. But very few of us, God knows, are perfect enough to be held forth as patterns. Men of strict and punctilious virtue in private life, will often allow themselves very reprehensible liberties in their public conduct. The temptations there, are much stronger; and the sense of duty is usually weaker than in other situations. At most, however, a man's example will justify those only who follow the virtues he practises, not those who neglect the duties which he never practised. If the men you affect to imitate are decent, temperate, and charitable; be decent, temperate, and charitable, like them; but be not, like them, corrupt and servile; imitate them no longer, when the only reasonable motive of imitation ceases.

In describing the causes of public unhappiness, I mean not to censure, or to encourage

encourage the cenfure, of public characters. It is our bufinefs to ftate the principles, and trace the limits of duty, in every rank of life. God forbid we fhould fo far degrade our character as to mix malevolence and abufe with the facred truths we deliver! There are too many always ready to watch and expofe human infirmities. But, perhaps a ferious word, pointed with truth, and uttered with tendernefs, may dart fudden light into a mifguided underftanding, and leave it ftartled and aftonifhed at the magnitude of its own crimes. It may be neceffary to touch only a few hearts, to fave a whole people; and whatever probability may lie againft the fuccefs, charity, in fo good a caufe, will wifh to make the experiment.

Inftead of continuing fuch reflections as thefe, you may, perhaps, rather think it proper for me to give the reafon of dwelling so long on so unusual a subject.—My reason is, that it is incumbent upon us to explain the whole doctrine of our Saviour.

It is the duty of our profession to preserve the everlasting gospel whole and undivided; and to teach it entire. Now the duties of public life, considered in their single acts, are by far the most important of all, and if they are never taught, or never taught clearly and honestly (and much more if they are disguised, dissembled, or complimented away), is it to be wondered at that they should be less understood, and worse obeyed, than any other of our obligations?—Add to this, that all the parts of our religion have a mutual dependance. It is necessary you should know the duties of governors and rulers, that you may be able to treat, with accuracy, the duties of subjects. From the nature and end of
their

their office and powers, arise the obligation and the limits of our obedience.

Some have observed, and with an appearance of truth; that since the Christian religion has prevailed, there have not been those great efforts of public spirit, those noble sacrifices to the interest of their country, which shone with so much lustre in the days of Grecian and Roman liberty. Without enquiring how the fact stands; I will boldly affirm, that the religion delivered to us in the gospel is not the cause of it. I appeal to you who study the scriptures daily;—What instructions do you there meet with but such as tend to the peace, and improvement, and happiness of mankind? When our Saviour would comprize our whole duty to man in one short, general expression, he commands us to love our neighbour; and in the parable of the good Samaritan, he extends the

meaning

meaning of the word neighbour, with great wisdom and precision, to all whom we can be useful to, or who can be useful to us. Temperance, self-denial, meekness, and humility, long-suffering, gentleness, kindness, and brotherly love; every thing that tends to recommend and endear us to one another, are the lessons repeated in almost every page. The whole world, to the eye of a Christian, appears as one great republic, united, under the law of kindness, in one common interest, or rather as one universal family, consisting of kindred and brethren, enjoying the common blessings of life under the wise administration of the Father of angels and men; and as being co-heirs of all the glorious hopes that are to be satisfied in a better world. Now, under such a dispensation as this, what room can we find for a government by force, administered only for the

the benefit of a few, at the expence of their brethren; much less of a government by corruption, *i. e* by discouraging every virtue, and disobeying every law, that Christ has given us? Such notions and such practices as these, in such a system as ours, are totally inadmissible. The only kind of government that is compatible with the clearest tenor of the gospel, is not an unhappy intercourse between force and arbitrary will, on one side; and terror and servility on the other; but an exercise of a mild, rational, and useful authority over a willing people; the integrity of a good steward, joined with the tenderness of a parent. Good government is not an exemption from the duties of the gospel, but a continual exercise of them.

It is very far from my thoughts to wish you to perplex your hearers with political controversies; or to enter into the local

intrigues

intrigues of confiderable families; and to take an active part in the management of elections. Nothing, in my opinion, is more inconfiftent with that decency of character, which unlefs we fupport, our inftructions will lofe their weight. Yet I am not ignorant that by fuch methods fome unworthy men have found means to rife, even in the church; but they meet with very little refpect, even from thofe who employ them, and I publicly declare that this kind of merit fhall entitle no one to any of the rewards that are in my difpofal. Should any one, however, chufe to engage in a ferious ftudy of the nature and formation of government, I cannot poffibly reprehend him for purfuing a path, where Mr. Hooker, with fo much wifdom and honour, has led the way. Indeed, the principles of good government, which is the moft effectual art yet known of making

ing men happy, are a study by no means unsuitable to our sacred function. Nor would I too roughly censure those who hunt after public happiness in the fields of invention (the only scene, I fear, where she is to be found in her perfect state), and amuse themselves with the enchanting dreams of young and virtuous minds, concerning imaginary states and kingdoms, where all is peace and felicity.

Such notions may raise expectations of improvement and happiness, which a corrupt people is very ill prepared to realize; but these harmless errors are too soon corrected by the rough experience of the world. Still let our minds be constantly exercised as far as our duties and our cares will permit, either in acquiring or communicating knowledge. Our profession abounds in leisure; and it is laudable to fill up the intervals of duty with every kind

of

of liberal enquiry.—This, if I do not flatter myself, has long been the singular character and merit of the National Clergy; and we ought not to suffer so high an honour to perish in our hands. They have taught their countrymen not only religion but science, and the principles of many useful and liberal arts. From the seeds of knowledge, which, by their instructions and society, have been scattered over the whole kingdom; have arisen, in some measure, that strong sense and just discernment of things, which have long distinguished the natives of this island; and, perhaps, in their time, no qualities have contributed more to that imperial wealth and greatness, which, at present, we can only remember.

We shall not do justice to the national prudence and merit of our ancestors, unless we acknowledge that they, in the most
ignorant

ignorant ages, with unwearied spirit, preserved, established, and defined the rights and liberties of the commons; that is of men in general; while their princes and nobles were employing their little passions and talents in contending for power, or abusing it. Our ancestors, when they knew little else, knew that it was not their interest to be oppressed, nor to leave it in the power of any man to oppress them. I will not hesitate to affirm that, from our legal constitution, which was gradually formed by the unexampled attention of our predecessors to the public good; may be collected a more useful and practical knowledge of government, than from all the abstract reasonings of the wisest men. Go, therefore, to the rock from whence you and your fathers, with all their virtues, were hewn; call to mind the good old usages, the laws and manners, and

principles

principles of your forefathers; thofe original moulds in which the noble character of an Englifhman was formed. The Conftitution which they have delivered to us, feems to have been rather the growth of time and nature, than the work of human invention. It acquired ftrength and form from the flow fuggeftions of fenfe and ufe, to a people in all circumftances attentive to their true interefts. It followed the changes of power, manners, and property; and every change was an improvement. Law was then employed to regifter the dictates of nature and experience; and that conformity to the prefent actual ftate of things in which confifts the virtue of all human eftablifhments, was preferved in the government of this country, by the living wifdom of the judges and the legiflature, under the filent controul of a free, armed, and vigilant people. Such

Such a wise and solid institution took deep root in the minds and hearts of men, and made this island happy for ages; even long after the commanding spirit and genius that formed it was departed from us. We may challenge all the annals of universal history to produce, in any ancient or modern state, a period of public prosperity and private freedom, and happiness, equal to what this nation has seen in the reigns that have passed since the Revolution. Ours was then the age and the country in which a wise man would have chosen to live. Let us often refresh our weary minds with the memory of those golden days, when we enjoyed all the blessings of nature, and all the improvements of mankind, in full measure and security; and had nothing to fear from our enemies or our rulers. All speculative forms of government are mere futility,

when

when compared with this found and folid experience of our anceftors. Let us therefore preferve in our hearts a religious veneration for that nobleft work of human wifdom, the Britifh Conftitution: but it more efpecially behoves us, in the day of danger and adverfity, to acquaint ourfelves with the large foundations of juftice, natural equality, and good-will to man, on which it was built. All the calamities of the people, and their rulers, in different periods, have been uniformly owing to fome unwife deviations from this great law of public happinefs.

We are an extravagant race, that have loft all that the virtue of our fathers had gained and faved for us. Let us, however, yet remember the good habits and wife principles, that made them great and happy: let us make the knowledge of them, at leaft, our own, and carefully preferve preserve it as the most precious inheritance we can now leave to our children. I trust I shall be forgiven by the lovers of their country, for this digression in its praise. It is pleasant to ruminate over her old virtues and glories, as on the worth and excellence of departed friends, who shared the best pleasures of our happiest days.

Allow me also to observe, that these reflections are not so foreign to our office and profession as they may at first appear: for, perhaps, the surest method we can take to preserve and propagate the pure religion we profess, is to preserve our free Constitution. The great advantage our religion has above all others, consists in its being true, which renders it sure of gaining by examination and enquiry. Now, every free state promotes freedom of enquiry; and freedom of enquiry is the most certain rule that God and nature have taught us for the discovery of truth. It is evident that Christianity flourishes no where so kindly, nor produces such excellent fruits, as under free governments. Religion itself can find no nobler seat upon earth than the heart of a freeman.

And if, at any time, the ministers of religion have lent the support of their authority to the worst of governments, it is not that religion is of itself favourable to arbitrary power, but that arbitrary power too often corrupts religion.

One caution more there is, which I look upon as rather proper for me to mention, than necessary for you to hear. It is that the most warm and ardent regard for the public, should never make us neglect either to teach or practise the duties of private life. For, to consider things fairly, those duties are, to every man, the most immediate and efficient causes of happiness.

Let

# CHARGE III.

Let public affairs be ever so prosperous, yet a man cannot be happy who lives at variance with his neighbours, or, through want of natural affection, neither performs the offices, nor relishes the enjoyments of domestic life. Private duties are the universal duties of every man, and he who has not discharged them, is in right, and ought to be in fact, utterly disqualified for the management of all public affairs; for the holding any place of trust or profit Government ought to be the employment of good men exclusively, none else can possibly be fit for it, I mean of such good men who think that he who commands them to love their neighbour, commands them also to love their country. Strange as these maxims may appear in our days, I do assure you they are not owing to my ignorance of the world, and its present opinions, but to the long observation of what that unhappy world has suffered by the neglect of them.

The substance of the doctrine I have endeavoured to explain may be comprehended in a few intelligible words. The manifest design of the Christian religion is to procure the improvement and happiness of man. The precepts of it are universal and obligatory on all, on princes as well as their subjects Meekness, patience, humility, and self-denial are the virtues common to both. In the practice of these, and of every other duty, the same prudence and good sense are to be used; the same considerations of time and place, the same attention to the characters of men, and the situation of things which we think it so necessary to employ in the conduct of our great temporal concerns. To suppose any exemptions from these duties in favor of the greatest, is to suppose what is evidently contrary to the intention, the wisdom, and the character of our great Lawgiver. That would be to undo his own work; to render his own divine law of none effect. If you ask me by what authority unjust rulers are to be punished, I can only answer, that history and experience tell us that they seldom escape punishment; and that they who transgress the laws of God, and are injurious to their fellow creatures, have every thing to fear from God and man. There is a provision in the constitution of nature, in the judgments of God, and the passions and instincts of men that will rectify this almost universal defect of civil government; and not suffer the blackest of all crimes to pass unpunished. From this great, universal, and inviolable obligation on all the sons of men to promote the general happiness by the practice of the gospel virtues, I will take upon me to infer, and I think with the strongest evidence, that the religion of Jesus, which I, his unworthy servant, have endeavoured to describe, and which I exhort you to preach, is not only holy, and wise, and just, and good, but is also the most public-spirited religion; the most favorable to civil liberty, the most beneficial to states and kingdoms, as well as individuals, which has ever yet appeared upon earth.

# CHARGE IV.

Delivered in the Year 1782.

---

IN the charge I delivered to you at my last general visitation, I thought it became me to take such notice of the melancholy situation of publick affairs, and to treat them with such a religious turn of thought as was suitable to men of our profession. Though there was then much reason for unfavorable suspicions, which have since arisen to a greater degree of certainty than we could have wished, yet I did not presume to censure any particular set of men, but endeavoured to give a plain description

tion of the duties incumbent upon all men in high office, who are intrusted with the direction of publick affairs. How far these duties had been performed or neglected I left to the judgment of those who had observed their conduct, and the benefit or mischief accruing from it. While the event of things was undetermined, there was prudence and charity in such caution as this. But after the whole nation have declared their sense of the misery and ruin that had well nigh overwhelmed them; we may now with freedom, and yet with decency, profess our honest opinions of of men and things. Yet even now, instead of turning our thoughts to the causes and the authors of our misfortunes; I would rather chuse to congratulate you on the fortunate change, which partly experience and the conviction of our own follies, but principally that all-wise Providence,

dence, which is always the truest friend of mankind, has wrought for us. The very men the people had wished for, who had lamented and felt their grievances, who knew their sufferings, and the language of their hearts, are the men that are now intrusted with the management of their affairs. We have already received some agreeable proofs that we have not been mistaken in our choice. Much of that profusion and extravagance which increased the burthen of the publick, and rendered it to a generous mind more irksome to bear, has been removed and suppressed They have gone farther than the cure of temporary evils, and have had the courage, with a wise and steady hand, to probe our wounds to the bottom. They have had the courage to attack that system of corruption, which other ministers have made use of as the necessary method of

doing

doing bufinefs; without which government could not be carried on. Yet with concern I am forced to own, that diffentions have taken place among the men to whom we are looking for fafety. But as we know the goodnefs of their characters, let us hope that they differ with that temper and integrity of heart which good men will preferve in all fituations, and may their contentions only make them ftrive who fhall be foremoft in the fervice of their country. Where men are honeft, something good and ufeful will enter into all they do, and even their ambition turn to the fervice of the publick.

I am fenfible that in treating this fubject, I am forced to introduce a language that is new and unufual on fuch occafions; and, in general, that whatever comes under the name of politicks, is confidered as unfuitable to our profeffion. And fo much indeed

indeed I most readily acknowledge, that it does not become the clergy to take an active part in the management of elections, or to enter into the intrigues of party; and much less does it become us to flatter the great; to foment the pride and the ambition of princes, and by extolling their power and sovereignty, to tempt them to use what was trusted to them for the good of the people, to their hurt and mischief. But then, on the other hand, it is not only allowable, but it is a clear and important part of our office, as ministers of the gospel, to explain distinctly what duties are expected from men in all the different ranks of life. And we must never forget, that all the various ranks and orders of men are connected together, and give and receive mutual assistances; " for we are members one of another." Men in the most elevated stations, who are appointed

pointed to act for the good of the whole, have their duties affigned to them, as well as the meaneft; and it is the intereft of every one of their fellow-fubjects, that thofe duties fhould be clearly taught and faithfully difcharged. For it is the conduct of the governing part of mankind that muft produce the fafety and happinefs of the reft, it depends, upon their right behaviour that we ourfelves may be enabled to lead quiet and peaceable lives in all godlinefs and honefty. But having formerly explained, with great integrity and the beft judgment that I am poffeft of, the duties that ftatefmen owe to the publick, and having now the happinefs to be placed under an Adminiftration beloved by the people, and profeffing to govern by the good old principles, which we feared had departed from us; but are now, thank God, returned, and appear in their full force

force and evidence; instead of enquiring farther into the duty of our governors, it rather becomes us at the present hour to consider what are the duties that our country requires from ourselves, from every one of us as we are subjects, as we are fellow-citizens, as we are Britons.

In all countries, wherever government is established, it is the duty of every private person to obey that man, or assembly of men, that are intrusted by the people with the power of making laws for the good of the whole. This obligation arises from the very nature of government itself, which would be of no effect if those who live under it were not obliged to obey it. And, indeed, it must be allowed, that under the worst and most arbitrary governments, there generally subsisted many good laws, which their subjects were in conscience bound to submit to. Even bad
princes

princes think it necessary to secure the persons and properties of their people against the injuries which they are disposed to offer to one another; and there are many useful regulations for the internal order and conveniences of the state, and its defence and security against foreign enemies, which are equally adopted by governments, whether good or bad, though not with the same choice and prudence. Now to these regulations, which are evidently intended for the benefit of the whole society, all men, in all countries, and under all governments, are alike obliged to submit: it is a duty we owe to our neighbours, our friends, and our countrymen, as well as to our rulers.

But then it becomes a question how far it may be obligatory upon us to obey our rulers in matters of a different sort, especially in instances where their commands are

are very unreasonable, and very oppressive. In the first place, let us trust St. Paul, and the reason of our own minds; and believe that they are the ministers of God for our good and indeed it would be difficult to assign any other cause for such an institution that is suitable to the goodness of God, or the wants and the prudence of man If, then, they should totally pervert the ends of their appointment, and become a terror to good works, and the abettors and encouragers of whatever is evil; it would certainly become criminal, or at least not obligatory, to render that obedience to them which they would be apt to expect. For, contracts in all dealings amongst men are dissolved, when the conditions are violated on which they were made. But as men are of different dispositions, and as our rulers, like other men, may have a great mixture of good and bad in their characters, it may become difficult to determine how far we are to submit, where laws unjust and oppressive, are intermingled with such as are useful and good.

Here, also, let your conduct be directed by the instructions you meet with in Scripture; and where those fail, or are not sufficiently clear, by the reason and light of your own minds; consider, in every instance, what Prudence, what Justice, and what Charity require of you. As long as you follow such excellent guides, you will never deviate far from the right way, and under their influence you will easily perceive what obedience you are to pay to civil government, and what duties you owe to your country. And this is much more easily understood, in cases like our own; where the wisdom of the nation has prescribed such limits to the power of

their

their princes, and exacted such conditions from them as they cannot transgress, without shaking the foundations of that allegiance on which their sovereignty is built. Happy is that people, which has thus secured their persons and properties, and the enjoyment of their rights, from the arbitrary will of man. And it is not only their interest, but their duty to preserve entire those noble privileges which their fathers have delivered to them, and which their children claim as their inheritance.

It is certainly not a grateful office to lay open the shame and dishonour of our country; but, it nearly concerns every one of us to know by what means the ruin, which we have hardly yet escaped, was brought so near to us. It is now generally known, and unwillingly acknowledged by those, whose interest would prompt them to conceal, it that the moſt unlimited corruption has prevailed in the general management of publick affairs, all the offices of Government, places and penſions, the dignities in the church, the important poſts in the law; all the immenſe patronage which the people have intruſted to the Crown to be employed as the reward of merit, or to provide for the publick ſervice, by filling every department with able and upright officers; all this and more, together with all the hopes, and deſires and paſſions, which they who have every thing to give, can raiſe in the corrupt and credulous heart of man, all this and every other art and inſtrument were employed to carry into execution thoſe ſchemes, which have diſpoſed of the whole intereſt and property of this unhappy country, without meaſure and without account, till hardly any thing is left. And what is

painful

painful to think of, the larger the burthens that were laid upon us the more we were defrauded, and the more pernicious the meafures, the greater fums were neceffary to prevail on interefted men to fupport them. We had an empire, but, it is now broken and feparated. We had colonies of ineftimable value for their commerce, their affiftance, and their fidelity: but now their power is acting againft us, and their wealth and trade are enriching our bittereft enemies. We had wealth and manufactures, but our wealth is gone, and our induftry fickens and declines. A few years ago, rents were high, and improvements were carried on with fpirit; I need not tell you, who hear me, what is the cafe at prefent; now that your lands have loft near half their value. In exchange for all thefe loffes, what have we gained but a load of enormous debt and infupportable taxes; and such a combination of powerful enemies against us, that even the bravery and the victories of our countrymen cannot long save us, and what terms of peace we can hope to obtain, must depend upon the will of the powerful and exasperated nations we are contending with. But to what end may many of you, who hear me, say, is all this singular disquisition on the state of publick affairs? Believe me, it is not from any pleasure I take in introducing what is called politicks into a place where it ought very seldom to appear, nor do I think it a grateful employment, to enumerate and dwell upon the calamities of our country but my design and my wishes are, to make you truly sensible how much the safety and happiness, even of private men, depend upon the manner in which they are governed.

The

## CHARGE IV.

The very essence of virtue and vice arises from the good and harm that men do in the world, and the knowledge of our duties themselves, is collected from a due consideration of the common interest. How great, then, must be that guilt which has brought this kingdom from the glorious state, which even the young may remember, to the condition in which we now find it. Yet I neither censure, nor acquit, those who were trusted till very lately with the management of publick affairs. It is the duty of their successors to let the people know how much they have been injured.

If we lived under an arbitrary prince, he, indeed, though no conditions were prescribed to him by his people, would still be bound to govern them by the rules of justice and humanity. The powers that be, are ordained of God, and God never

gave to any man a power, I mean a lawful power, to commit injuftice and wrong. Such a power would be an evident contradiction in terms. But ftill, where the people have left the whole management of their interefts to the difcretion of one man, there private perfons have no choice, but to fubmit, unlefs the oppreffion becomes fo enormous and evident as to convince a majority that refiftance is become neceffary to felf-prefervation. But where men have had the wifdom, and happily for us our fathers were fo wife, as, to require their princes to govern according to fuch conditions of law and juftice as were at firft agreed upon, there it becomes not only the intereft, but the duty of every man, as far as his power and influence extends, to fee that thofe conditions are punctually obferved and complied with. Now, parliaments, efpecially that part of
them

them which reprefents the people, were inftituted to fhare the fupreme power with the prince, and to be a check upon an authority that would otherwife be arbitrary. But that power, which is intended to check and reftrain another power, muft neceffarily be fuppofed independent of that which it is to reftrain, and yet from the want of a due regard to fo very obvious a truth, have proceeded all the publick miferies we have felt, and all the dangers we fear. This could not have happened, if private men had always required, in the choice of their reprefentatives, that integrity and goodnefs of character, which common fenfe will teach us to look for, in thofe to whom we entruft every thing that is valuable. But our anceftors were honeft and carelefs, our fathers faw the growth and progrefs of corruption, but not feeling much harm from

from an evil that made its advances by gentle degrees, they little thought that what they neglected as a trifle, would be the misery and destruction of their children. We, however, should be of all men the most inexcusable, if, under the immediate sense and experience of almost every publick evil, we should neglect any lawful means to shake off that load of sin and misery which almost overwhelms us. I wish not, my brethren, to inflame your passions, I serve no faction; I pay servile court to no man. I speak the language of truth and soberness, of piety and virtue. I give utterance to those sentiments, which are suggested in far more significant terms than mine, by the wrongs, and the distresses of our country.

The time, perhaps, is soon approaching, when you will be trusted once more with the choice of your representatives. Whenever

Whenever it comes, give the world a proof of your own integrity, by votes and recommendations in favour of intelligent and worthy men, men of independent fortunes; but not raised by the plunder of the publick, who have shewn their love for their country by their hatred of corruption. Nor is it sufficient to chuse men wise and honest, but, considering the weakness of our common nature, we ought to employ the most just and probable methods to keep them so. We ought to favour and support the endeavours of many worthy men, to preserve the integrity of their representatives, by not trusting them with power too long, by transferring the right of election, from the shameless inhabitants of small boroughs, without property or principle, to great commercial towns, or to larger districts; and, as much as possible, to place the power

of

of chusing our lawgivers in the hands of honest and independent men, who have an interest not to abuse it. Above all, we should encourage those plans which tend to restrain the expences, and lessen the profits, and the frauds of Government; and to guard against the growth of that incroaching power, from which neither we, nor our fathers, have been sufficiently able to secure ourselves. But some affect to be alarmed at these proceedings, as dangerous innovations, and a change in the constitution. That it is a change must be allowed, but a change that we ought to wish and pray for, a change from rottenness and disease, to vigour, health, and gladness. Changes and alterations are the natural steps which the mind of man makes in its progress towards improvement, they arise from the wisdom of experience. The constitution itself is

little

little more than a collection of such changes and alterations as our forefathers found neceffary to be made in the form of their government, and why fhould not we be allowed to watch over our own fafety, as well as they.

The order, conftancy, and beauty of the creation itfelf is preferved by thofe periodical and falutary changes, by which the whole frame of nature is in a manner renewed and invigorated. But after all, what are the alarming changes thefe men are afraid of? Suppofe that they were all to take place, the full effect of them could amount to no more than to give the nation a chance of having more honeft reprefentatives than we have hitherto been bleft with. Now, if honefty was really that noxious weed, which fome men feem to think it, yet it does not take root fo deep, nor fpread fo faft, that we need be under any fear of its over-running

the

the land. It is remarkable, that in our late shameful days, when new sources of corruption were daily opening, and influence was grown irresistable; no such apprehensions of danger appeared from the same quarter, honesty it seems is the only thing we have to fear. Sure no man can seriously think that a change, which will only make us more honest, is a change to be afraid of, for if it does not make us honester, it is no change at all. Yet I ought not to conceal from you, my brethren, that we have been told from an unexpected place, and from no mean authority, that the principles and conduct we recommend, are not the way to preferment. Perhaps we cannot dispute the assertion. Those who tell us so, certainly knew the way to preferment better than we. But if the endeavour to serve our country does not lead to preferment; it may

may ftill be a good road, and perhaps may lead to fomething better. It may lead to felf-fatisfaction, to a good name, to the honour of our religion, and to the happinefs of our brethren.

I know of no precept in the Gofpel that either teaches or recommends to us the art of rifing in courts, but 'they enjoin us moft exprefsly to lift up our hearts above the pomps and vanities of this wicked world, and, with a true greatnefs of mind, to defpife them.

Our proper ftate is a life of learning, reflection, and retirement, adapted to the improvement of ourfelves, as our employment is to the fervice and inftruction of our neighbours. A competency in the middle ftate of life, which is undoubtedly the happieft, is what a common fhare of merit in our profeffion is almoft fure of attaining. Indeed, I never yet knew a re-

fpectable

spectable clergyman that was totally neglected by the world. Let us, therefore, venture to trust the care of our fortunes to the disposal of our Almighty Father. He is the never-failing friend of virtuous men, and all good things are in his patronage And let us not, for any fallacious hopes of advantage, those waking dreams of worldly men, neglect to preach so useful and essential a doctrine as the love of our country and the duty we owe to it, which, in the eye of mere reason, and in the sense of those worthies, who, in all ages, have eminently served mankind, is the most binding and sacred of all duties. Forget not that all which this poor country has suffered for the last seven years, all that we still feel, and all the unknown evils we may justly fear, will have been owing to the general neglect of this most sacred duty. To the practice of this duty was

owing

owing the good established government which produced all the singular blessings which our fathers enjoyed, and which gave them that honourable superiority over other nations which their degenerate sons have lost. It is surely worth while to consider how a duty so useful to mankind, and so respectable in itself, should have been so little regarded, and held as something distinct and separate from our religious obligations. Some Divines have thought proper seriously to enquire into the cause why no mention is made in the Gospel of the duties of friendship, or the love of our country, without the latter of which no state can be free, and without the former no private man can be happy. If the charge was just, the omission would be unpardonable. But they seem not to have enough attended to the large and comprehensive sense in which the divine law every where abounds. When we are taught to love our neighbour, to do good to all men, and to perfect ourselves in that love which is the fulfilling of the law; our Saviour expects that we should use the judgment he has given us, and the prudence we have acquired by living in the world, in obeying his precepts so as to answer his intentions. It is impossible, perhaps, that by any effort of ours, we can serve or benefit all mankind. At least, that is an honour reserved only for a few, who may be considered as the favourites of heaven. The influence of our limited powers cannot hope to reach so far. But the nearest approach we can make towards filling up so immense a description of our duty, is by performing what we owe to our country, that great society which is the largest portion of mankind with whom we are connected, from whom we can derive any benefit; or to which we can pay any service. This is to manifest the love of our neighbour, and to do good to all men, in the most literal sense, and to the fullest extent that our faculties can reach. To serve our country is the nearest approach we can make to the service of mankind.

If you ask me in what instances this duty is to be chiefly exerted; I answer, in the first place, and at all seasons, by behaving with sense, integrity, and goodness, in your respective stations, and by instructing your neighbours to do the same. Make yourselves good men, and you can hardly avoid being good citizens; and you serve your country very essentially if you qualify yourselves, and encourage others, to serve it. This, perhaps, in seasons of peace and quiet, is all the duty that your country expects from private men. But, in of public danger and calamity, when there is either strong proof, or just and general suspicion of wrong management, it may then become necessary for every man, as far as his power and influence extend, to inform himself of the state of things; and join in such petitions, and other constitutional measures, as may carry the uncorrupted sense of the people to the Throne, and make our rulers forget, for a while, their greatness, and remember their obligations. That sense, which is the language of facts, and the feelings of men, is almost universally right; but it rises to the force and evidence of demonstration, when it remonstrates against things wrong in themselves, particularly against that undue influence and corruption which appear in so many seducing forms, and which it is not to be expected that common good characters should resist

Our

Our business is, by preaching and instruction, to make men honest and good; but we all know how little our endeavours can avail when strong temptations and interested motives are used to counteract them. What then have we to hope should all the terrors, and profits, and promises, of government, be employed to make men act against their principles? Nothing, therefore, is of more consequence, even to religion itself, than that the powers of government, which are of such extensive and irresistible efficacy, should be placed in virtuous hands, and we cannot serve our country more effectually than by employing our wishes, our approbation, and our warmest endeavours, in the advancement of so good a work. Especially, let us not suffer good men to think that the direction of public affairs is a matter of indifference, and that politics have no concern with religion.

ligion. Perhaps there is no opinion that has been more inftrumental than this in bringing on our public misfortunes. When good men have been perfuaded by the converfation and example of many in high rank, and of decent characters, that a man is juftified by a fpirit of honour and confiftency in fupporting the meafures of his party, be they right or wrong; there could not be a more fuccefsful contrivance to make them guilty of the moft immoral, unjuft, and pernicious actions, to make them the moft ufeful tools that ambition and wickednefs can work with. Remember what is the fenfe of the Apoftle on a fubject like this. He that doth righteoufnefs is righteous. Our underftanding is the moft valuable talent that God has given us, and of the moft extenfive ufe. Employ that talent, whenever you take a part or pafs a judgment on public meafures.
Watch

Watch the consequences of things, and observe the characters of men; and then act upon the fullest information you can get, with the same attention and sincerity that you chuse to exert in your most important private affairs.

I hope my brethren will forgive me for having insisted so largely on a duty, from the neglect of which, every one who hears me is a sufferer; and, perhaps, our dear country, whose name used to be the pride and delight of our hearts, is, at this moment, perishing. Let them do me the justice to believe, that I speak the language of an honest man; of one who loves and respects his clergy, who loves his diocese, and who loves his country.

A

SPEECH,

INTENDED TO HAVE BEEN SPOKEN

ON THE

BILL

FOR

ALTERING THE CHARTERS

OF THE

COLONY OF MASSACHUSETT'S BAY.

# ADVERTISEMENT.

---

THE Author of the following Speech might justify his manner of publishing it by very great authorities. Some of the noblest pieces of eloquence, the world is in possession of, were not spoken on the great occasions they were intended to serve, and seemed to have been preserved merely from the high sense that was entertained of their merit.

The present performance appears in public from humbler but juster motives:

tives: from the great national importance of the subject, from a very warm desire and some faint hope of serving our country, by suggesting a few of the useful truths which great men are apt to overlook.

The Author has abstained most religiously from personal reflections. He has censured no man, and therefore hopes he has offended no man. He feels most sensibly the misfortune of differing from many of those whom he wishes to live and act with; and from some of as much virtue and ability as this kingdom affords. But there are also great authorities on the other side; and the greatest authority can never

persuade

persuade him, that it is better to extort by force, what he thinks may be gained more surely by gentle means.

He looks upon power as a coarse and mechanical instrument of government, and holds the use of it to be particularly dangerous to the relation that subsists between a mother-country and her colonies. In such a case he doubts whether any point ought to be pursued, which cannot be carried by persuasion, by the sense of a common interest, and the exercise of a moderate authority. He thinks it unnecessary to lay down the limits of sovereignty and obedience, and more unnecessary to fight for them. If we can but restore

that

that mutual regard and confidence, which formerly governed our whole intercourse with our colonies, particular cases will easily provide for themselves. He acts the part of the truest patriot in this dangerous crisis, whether he lives at London or at Boston, who pursues sincerely the most lenient and conciliating measures; and wishes to restore the public peace by some better method than the slaughter of our fellow-citizens.

# A
# SPEECH,
### &c. &c. &c.

---

IT is of such great importance to compose or even to moderate the dissentions, which subsist at present between our unhappy country and her colonies, that I cannot help endeavouring, from the faint prospect I have of contributing something to so good an end, to overcome the inexpressible reluctance I feel at uttering my thoughts before the most respectable of all audiences.

The true object of all our deliberations on this occasion, which I hope we shall never

never lose sight of, is a full and cordial reconciliation with North America. Now I own, my Lords, I have many doubts whether the terrors and punishments, we hang out to them at present, are the surest means of producing this reconciliation. Let us at least do this justice to the people of North America to own, that we can all remember a time when they were much better friends than at present to their mother country. They are neither our natural nor our determined enemies. Before the Stamp Act, we considered them in the light of as good subjects as the natives of any county in England.

It is worth while to enquire by what steps we first gained their affection, and preserved it so long; and by what conduct we have lately lost it. Such an enquiry may point out the means of restoring peace, and make the use of force unnecessary

against

against a people, whom I cannot yet forbear to consider as our brethren.

It has always been a most arduous task to govern distant provinces, with even a tolerable appearance of justice. The viceroys and governors of other nations are usually temporary tyrants, who think themselves obliged to make the most of their time, who not only plunder the people, but carry away their spoils, and dry up all the sources of commerce and industry. Taxation in their hands, is an unlimited power of oppression: but in whatever hands the power of taxation is lodged, it implies and includes all other powers. Arbitrary taxation is plunder authorised by law: it is the support and the essence of tyranny; and has done more mischief to mankind, than those other three scourges from heaven, famine, pestilence, and the sword. I need not carry your Lordships out of your own knowledge, or out of your own dominions, to make you conceive what misery this right of taxation is capable of producing in a provincial government. We need only recollect, that our countrymen in India have, in the space of five or six years, in virtue of this right, destroyed, starved, and driven away more inhabitants from Bengal, than are to be found at present in all our American Colonies, more than all those formidable numbers which we have been nursing up for the space of 200 years, with so much care and success, to the astonishment of all Europe. This is no exaggeration, my Lords, but plain matter of fact, collected from the accounts sent over by Mr. Hastings, whose name I mention with honour and veneration. And I must own, such accounts have very much lessened the pleasure I used to feel in thinking myself

myself an Englishman. We ought surely not to hold our colonies totally inexcusable for wishing to exempt themselves from a grievance, which has caused such unexampled devastation; and, my Lords, it would be too disgraceful to ourselves, to try so cruel an experiment more than once. Let us reflect, that before these innovations were thought of, by following the line of good conduct which had been marked out by our ancestors, we governed North America with mutual benefit to them and ourselves. It was a happy idea, that made us first consider them rather as instruments of commerce than as objects of government. It was wise and generous to give them the form and the spirit of our own constitution, an assembly in which a greater equality of representation has been preserved than at home, and councils and governors, such as were adapted to their situation, though they must be acknowledged to be very inferior copies of the dignity of this House, and the Majesty of the Crown.

But what is far more valuable than all the rest, we gave them liberty. We allowed them to use their own judgment in the management of their own interest. The idea of taxing them never entered our heads. On the contrary, they have experienced our liberality on many public occasions: we have given them bounties to encourage their industry, and have demanded no return but what every state exacts from its colonies, the advantages of an exclusive commerce, and the regulations that are necessary to secure it. We made requisitions to them on great occasions, in the same manner as our princes formerly asked benevolences of their subjects, and as nothing was asked but what was visibly for

for the public good, it was always granted; and they sometimes did more than we expected. The matter of right was neither disputed, nor even considered. And let us not forget that the people of New England were themselves, during the last war, the most forward of all in the national cause, that every year we voted them a considerable sum, in acknowledgment of their zeal and their services; that in the preceding war, they alone enabled us to make the treaty of Aix la Chapelle, by furnishing us with the only equivalent for the towns that were taken from our allies in Flanders; and that in times of peace, they alone have taken from us six times as much of our woollen manufactures, as the whole kingdom of Ireland. Such a colony, my Lords, not only from the justice, but from the gratitude we owe them, have a right to be heard in their defence, and if their crimes are not of the moſt inexpiable kind, I could almoſt ſay, they have a right to be forgiven

But in the times we ſpeak of, our public intercourſe was carried on with eaſe and ſatisfaction. We regarded them as our friends and fellow-citizens, and relied as much upon their fidelity as on the inhabitants of our own country They ſaw our power with pleaſure; for they conſidered it only as their protection. They inherited our laws, our language, and our cuſtoms, they preferred our manufactures, and followed our faſhions with a partiality, that ſecured our excluſive trade with them, more effectually than all the regulations and vigilance of the cuſtom-houſe. Had we ſuffered them to enrich us a little longer, and to grow a little richer themſelves, their men of fortune, like the Weſt-Indians, would undoubtedly have made

made this country their place of education and resort. For they looked up to England with reverence and affection, as to the country of their friends and ancestors. They esteemed and they called it their home, and thought of it as the Jews once thought of the Land of Canaan.

Now, my Lords, consider with yourselves what were the chains and ties that united this people to their mother-country, with so much warmth and affection, at so amazing a distance. The colonies of other nations have been discontented with their treatment, and not without sufficient cause, always murmuring at their grievances, and sometimes breaking out into acts of rebellion. Our subjects at home, with all their reasons for satisfaction, have never been entirely satisfied. Since the beginning of this century we have had two rebellions, several plots and conspiracies, and we ourselves have been witnesses to the most dangerous excesses of sedition. But the provinces in North America have engaged in no party, have excited no opposition; they have been utter strangers even to the name of Whig and Tory. In all changes, in all revolutions, they have quietly followed the fortunes, and submitted to the government of England.

Now let me appeal to your Lordships, as to men of enlarged and liberal minds, who have been led by your office and rank to the study of history. Can you find in the long succession of ages, in the whole extent of human affairs, a single instance, where distant provinces have been preserved in so flourishing a state, and kept at the same time in such due subjection to their mother country? My Lords, there is no instance, the case never existed before. It is perhaps the most singular phænomenon

menon in all civil history, and the cause of it well deserves your serious consideration. The true cause is, that a mother country never existed before, who placed her natives and her colonies on the same equal footing; and joined with them in fairly carrying on one common interest.

You ought to consider this, my Lords, not as a mere historical fact, but as a most important and invaluable discovery. It enlarges our ideas of the power and energy of good government beyond all former examples, and shews that it can act, like gravitation, at the greatest distances. It proves to a demonstration that you may have good subjects in the remotest corners of the earth, if you will but treat them with kindness and equity. If you have any doubts of the truth of this kind of reasoning, the experience we have had of a different kind will entirely remove them.

The

The good genius of our country had led us to the simple and happy method of governing freemen, which I have endeavoured to describe. Our ministers received it from their predecessors, and for some time continued to observe it, but without knowing its value. At length, presuming on their own wisdom, and the quiet disposition of the Americans, they flattered themselves that we might reap great advantages from their prosperity by destroying the cause of it. They chose in an unlucky hour to treat them as other nations have thought fit to treat their colonies, they threatened and they taxed them.

I do not now enquire whether taxation is matter of right; I only consider it as matter of experiment, for surely the art of government itself is founded on experience. I need not suggest what were the

the confequences of this change of meafures. The evils produced by it were fuch as we ftill remember and ftill feel. We fuffered more by our lofs of trade with them, than the wealth flowing in from India was able to recompenfe. The bankruptcy of the Eaft India Company may be fufficiently accounted for by the rapine abroad and the knavery at home; but it certainly would have been delayed fome years, had we continued our commerce with them in the fingle article of tea. But that and many other branches of trade have been diverted into other channels, and may probably never return intire to their old courfe. But what is worft of all, we have loft their confidence and friendfhip; we have ignorantly undermined the moft folid foundation of our own power.

In order to obferve the ftricteft impartiality,

tiality, it is but just for us to enquire what we have gained by these taxes as well as what we have lost. I am assured that out of all the sums raised in America the last year but one, if the expences are deducted, which the natives would else have discharged themselves, the net revenue paid into the Treasury to go in aid of the sinking fund, or to be employed in whatever public services parliament shall think fit, is eighty-five pounds. Eighty-five pounds, my Lords, is the whole equivalent we have received for all the hatred and mischief, and all the infinite losses this kingdom has suffered during that year in her disputes with North America. Money that is earned so dearly as this, ought to be expended with great wisdom and œconomy. My Lords, were you to take up but one thousand pounds more from North America upon the same terms,

terms, the nation itself would be a bankrupt. But the most amazing and the most alarming circumstance is still behind. It is that our case is so incurable, that all this experience has made no impression upon us. And yet, my Lords, if you could but keep these facts, which I have ventured to lay before you, for a few moments in your minds (supposing your right of taxation to be never so clear), yet I think you must necessarily perceive that it cannot be exercised in any manner that can be advantageous to ourselves or them. We have not always the wisdom to tax ourselves with propriety; and I am confident we could never tax a people at that distance, without infinite blunders, and infinite oppression. And to own the truth, my Lords, we are not honest enough to trust ourselves with the power of shifting our own burthens upon them. Allow me, therefore,

therefore, to conclude, I think, unanswerably, that the inconvenience and distress we have felt in this change of our conduct, no less than the ease and tranquillity we formerly found in the pursuit of it, will force us, if we have any sense left, to return to the good old path we trod in so long, and found it the way of pleasantness.

I desire to have it understood, that I am opposing no rights that our legislature may think proper to claim. I am only comparing two different methods of government. By your old rational and generous administration, by treating the Americans as your friends and fellow-citizens, you made them the happiest of human kind; and at the same time drew from them, by commerce, more clear profit than Spain has drawn from all its mines; and their growing numbers were

a daily-a daily-increasing addition to your strength. There was no room for improvement or alteration in so noble a system of policy as this. It was sanctified by time, by experience, by public utility. I will venture to use a bold language, my Lords, I will assert, that if we had uniformly adopted this equitable administration in all our distant provinces, as far as circumstances would admit, it would have placed this country, for ages, at the head of human affairs in every quarter of the world. My Lords, this is no visionary or chimerical doctrine. The idea of governing provinces and colonies by force is visionary and chimerical. The experiment has often been tried and it has never succeeded. It ends infallibly in the ruin of the one country or the other, or in the last degree of wretchedness.

If there is any truth, my Lords, in what
I have

I have said, and I most firmly believe it all to be true, let me recommend it to you to resume that generous and benevolent spirit in the discussion of our differences, which used to be the source of our union. We certainly did wrong in taxing them; when the Stamp Act was repealed, we did wrong in laying on other taxes, which tended only to keep alive a claim, that was mischievous, impracticable, and useless: We acted contrary to our own principles of liberty, and to the generous sentiments of our sovereign, when we defired to have their judges dependent on the crown for their stipends as well as their continuance. It was equally unwise to wish to make the governors independent of the people for their salaries. We ought to consider the governors, not as spies intrusted with the management of our interest, but as the servants of the people, recommended to
them

them by us. Our ears ought to be open to every complaint againſt the governors; but we ought not to ſuffer the governors to complain of the people. We have taken a different method, to which no ſmall part of our difficulties are owing. Our ears have been open to the governors and ſhut to the people. This muſt neceſſarily lead us to countenance the jobs of intereſted men, under the pretence of defending the rights of the crown. But the people are certainly the beſt judges whether they are well governed, and the crown can have no rights inconſiſtent with the happineſs of the people.

Now, my Lords, we ought to do what I have ſuggeſted, and many things more, out of prudence and juſtice, to win their affection, and to do them public ſervice. If we have a right to govern them, let us exert it for the true ends of government.

But, my Lords, what we ought to do, from motives of reason and justice, is much more than is sufficient to bring them to a reasonable accommodation. For thus, as I apprehend, stands the case. They petition for the repeal of an act of parliament, which they complain of as unjust and oppressive. And there is not a man amongst us, not the warmest friend of administration, who does not sincerely wish that act had never been made. In fact, they only ask for what we wish to be rid of. Under such a disposition of mind, one would imagine there could be no occasion for fleets and armies to bring men to a good understanding. But, my Lords, our difficulty lies in the point of honour. We must not let down the dignity of the mother country; but preserve her sovereignty over all the parts of the British Empire. This language has something in it that sounds pleasant to the

the ears of Englishmen, but is otherwise of little weight. For sure, my Lords, there are methods of making reasonable concessions, and yet without injuring our dignity. Ministers are generally fruitful in expedients to reconcile difficulties of this kind, to escape the embarrassments of forms, the competitions of dignity and precedency; and to let clashing rights sleep while they transact their business. Now, my Lords, on this occasion can they find no excuse, no pretence, no invention, no happy turn of language, not one colourable argument for doing the greatest service they can ever render to their country? It must be something more than incapacity that makes men barren of expedients at such a season as this. Do, but for once, remove this impracticable stateliness and dignity, and treat the matter with a little common sense and a little good humour, and our reconciliation would not be the work of an hour. But after all, my Lords, if there is any thing mortifying in undoing the errors of our ministers, it is a mortification we ought to submit to. If it was unjust to tax them, we ought to repeal it for their sakes, if it was unwise to tax them, we ought to repeal it for our own. A matter so trivial in itself as the three-penny duty upon tea, but which has given cause to so much national hatred and reproach, ought not to be suffered to subsist an unnecessary day. Must the interest, the commerce, and the union of this country and her colonies, be all of them sacrificed to save the credit of one imprudent measure of administration? I own I cannot comprehend that there is any dignity either in being in the wrong, or in persisting in it. I have known friendship preserved and affection gained, but I never knew dignity lost,

loſt, by the candid acknowledgment of an error. And, my Lords, let me appeal to your own experience of a few years backward (I will not mention particulars, because I would paſs no cenſures and revive no unpleaſant reflections) but I think every candid miniſter muſt own, that adminiſtration has ſuffered in more inſtances than one, both in intereſt and credit, by not chuſing to give up points, that could not be defended.

With regard to the people of Boſton, I am free to own that I neither approve of their riots nor their puniſhment. And yet if we inflict it as we ought, with a conſciouſneſs that we were ourſelves the aggreſſors, that we gave the provocation, and that their diſobedience is the fruit of our own imprudent and imperious conduct, I think the puniſhment cannot riſe to any great degree of ſeverity.

I own,

I own, my Lords, I have read the report of the Lords Committees of this House, with very different sentiments from those with which it was drawn up. It seems to be designed, that we should consider their violent measures and speeches, as so many determined acts of opposition to the sovereignty of England, arising from the malignity of their own hearts. One would think the mother country had been totally silent and passive in the progress of the whole affair. I, on the contrary, consider these violences as the natural effects of such measures as ours on the minds of freemen. And this is the most useful point of view, in which government can consider them. In their situation, a wise man would expect to meet with the strongest marks of passion and imprudence, and be prepared to forgive them. The first and easiest thing to be done is to correct our own errors;

errors; and I am confident we should find it the most effectual method to correct theirs. At any rate let us put ourselves in the right, and then, if we must contend with North America, we shall be unanimous at home, and the wise and the moderate there will be our friends. At present we force every North American to be our enemy, and the wise and moderate at home, and those immense multitudes, which must soon begin to suffer by the madness of our rulers, will unite to oppose them. It is a strange idea we have taken up, to cure their resentments by increasing their provocations, to remove the effects of our own ill conduct, by multiplying the instances of it. But the spirit of blindness and infatuation is gone forth. We are hurrying wildly on without any fixed design, without any important object. We pursue a vain phantom of unlimited sovereignty, which was not made for man, and reject the solid advantages of a moderate, useful, and intelligible authority. That just God, whom we have all so deeply offended, can hardly inflict a severer national punishment, than by committing us to the natural consequences of our own conduct. Indeed, in my opinion, a blacker cloud never hung over this island.

To reason consistently with the principles of justice and national friendship which I have endeavoured to establish, or rather to revive what was established by our ancestors, as our wisest rule of conduct for the government of America, I must necessarily disapprove of the bill before us, for it contradicts every one of them. In our present situation, every act of the legislature, even our acts of severity ought to be so many steps towards the reconciliation

tion we wish for. But to change the government of a people, without their consent, is the highest and most arbitrary act of sovereignty, that one nation can exercise over another. The Romans hardly ever proceeded to this extremity even over a conquered nation, till its frequent revolts and insurrections had made them deem it incorrigible. The very idea of it, implies a most total abject and slavish dependency in the inferior state. Recollect that the Americans are men of like passions with ourselves, and think how deeply this treatment must affect them. They have the same veneration for their charters, that we have for our Magna Charta, and they ought in reason to have greater. They are the title deeds to all their rights both public and private. What! my Lords, must these rights never acquire any legal assurance and stability? Can they derive no force

force from the peaceable poffeffion of near two hundred years? And muft the fundamental conftitution of a powerful ftate, be for ever fubject to as capricious alterations as you may think fit to make in the charters of a little mercantile company, or the corporation of a borough? This will undoubtedly furnifh matter for a more pernicious debate than has yet been moved. Every other colony will make the cafe its own. They will complain that their rights can never be afcertained, that every thing belonging to them depends upon our arbitrary will; and may think it better to run any hazard, than to fubmit to the violence of their mother country, in a matter in which they can fee neither moderation nor end.

But let us coolly enquire, what is the reafon of this unheard-of innovation. Is it to make them peaceable? My Lords,

it

it will make them mad. Will they be better governed if we introduce this change? Will they be more our friends? The least that such a measure can do, is, to make them hate us. And would to God, my Lords, we had governed ourselves with as much œconomy, integrity, and prudence as they have done. Let them continue to enjoy the liberty our fathers gave them. Gave them, did I say? They are coheirs of liberty with ourselves, and their portion of the inheritance has been much better looked after than ours. Suffer them to enjoy a little longer that short period of public integrity and domestic happiness, which seems to be the portion allotted by Providence to young rising states. Instead of hoping that their constitution may receive improvement from our skill in government, the most useful wish I can form in their favour

vour is, that heaven may long preserve them from our vices and our politics.

Let me add farther, that to make any changes in their government without their consent, would be to transgress the wisest rules of policy, and to wound our most important interests. As they increase in numbers and in riches, our comparative strength must lessen. In another age, when our power has begun to lose something of its superiority, we should be happy if we could support our authority by mutual good-will and the habit of commanding, but chiefly by those original establishments, which time and public honour might have rendered inviolable. Our posterity will then have reason to lament that they cannot avail themselves of those treasures of public friendship and confidence which our fathers had wisely hoarded up, and we are throwing away

It

It is hard, it is cruel, besides all our debts and taxes, and those enormous expences which are multiplying upon us every year, to load our unhappy sons with the hatred and curses of North America. Indeed, my Lords, we are treating posterity very scurvily. We have mortgaged all the lands, we have cut down all the oaks, we are now trampling down the fences, rooting up the seedlings and samplers, and ruining all the resources of another age. We shall send the next generation into the world, like the wretched heir of a worthless father, without money, credit, or friends; with a stripped, incumbered, and perhaps untenanted estate

Having spoke so largely against the principle of the bill, it is hardly necessary to enter into the merits of it. I shall only observe, that even if we had the consent of the people to alter their government, it would

would be unwise to make such alterations as these. To give the appointment of the governor and council to the crown; and the disposal of all places, even of the judges, and with a power of removing them, to the governor, is evidently calculated with a view to form a strong party in our favour. This I know has been done in other colonies; but still this is opening a source of perpetual discord, where it is our interest always to agree. If we mean any thing by this establishment, it is to support the governor and the council against the people, *i. e.* to quarrel with our friends, that we may please their servants This scheme of governing them by a party is not wisely imagined; it is much too premature, and, at all events, must turn to our disadvantage. If it fails, it will only make us contemptible; if it succeeds, it will make us odious. It is our interest to take very little part in their

their domestic administration of government, but purely to watch over them for their good. We never gained so much by North America as when we let them govern themselves, and were content to trade with them and to protect them. One would think, my Lords, there were some statute law, prohibiting us, under the severest penalties, to profit by experience.

My Lords, I have ventured to lay my thoughts before you, on the greatest national concern that ever came under your deliberation, with as much honesty as you will meet with from abler men, and with a melancholy assurance, that not a word of it will be regarded. And yet, my Lords, with your permission, I will waste one short argument more on the same cause, one that I own I am fond of, and which contains in it, what, I think, must affect every generous mind. My Lords, I look upon

North America as the only great nursery of freemen now left upon the face of the earth. We have seen the liberties of Poland and Sweden swept away, in the course of one year, by treachery and usurpation. The free towns in Germany are like so many dying sparks, that go out one after another, and which must all be soon extinguished under the destructive greatness of their neighbours. Holland is little more than a great trading company, with luxurious manners, and an exhausted revenue, with little strength, and with less spirit. Switzerland alone is free and happy within the narrow inclosure of its rocks and vallies. As for the state of this country, my Lords, I can only refer myself to your own secret thoughts. I am disposed to think and hope the best of public liberty. Were I to describe her according to my own ideas at present, I should say that she has a sickly countenance,

countenance, but I truſt ſhe has a ſtrong conſtitution.

But whatever may be our future fate, the greateſt glory that attends this country, a greater than any other nation ever acquired, is to have formed and nurſed up to ſuch a ſtate of happineſs, thoſe colonies whom we are now ſo eager to butcher. We ought to cheriſh them as the immortal monuments of our public juſtice and wiſdom; as the heirs of our better days, of our old arts and manners, and of our expiring national virtues. What work of art, or power, or public utility has ever equalled the glory of having peopled a continent without guilt or bloodſhed, with a multitude of free and happy common-wealths, to have given them the beſt arts of life and government; and to have ſuffered them under the ſhelter of our authority, to acquire in peace the skill to use them. In comparison of this, the policy of governing by influence, and even the pride of war and victory are dishonest tricks, and poor contemptible pageantry.

We seem not to be sensible of the high and important trust which Providence has committed to our charge. The most precious remains of civil liberty, that the world can now boast of, are lodged in our hands; and God forbid that we should violate so sacred a deposit. By enslaving your colonies, you not only ruin the peace, the commerce, and the fortunes of both countries, but you extinguish the fairest hopes, shut up the last asylum of mankind. I think, my Lords, without being weakly superstitious, that a good man may hope that Heaven will take part against the execution of a plan which seems big, not only with mischief, but impiety.

Let

Let us be content with the spoils and the destruction of the east. If your Lordships can see no impropriety in it, let the plunderer and the oppressor still go free. But let not the love of liberty be the only crime you think worthy of punishment. I fear we shall soon make it a part of our natural character, to ruin every thing that has the misfortune to depend upon us.

No nation has ever before contrived, in so short a space of time, without any war or public calamity (unless unwise measures may be so called) to destroy such ample resources of commerce, wealth and power, as of late were ours, and which, if they had been rightly improved, might have raised us to a state of more honourable and more permanent greatness than the world has yet seen.

Let me remind the noble Lords in administration, that before the stamp act, they had power sufficient to answer all the just ends of government, and they were all completely answered. If that is the power they want, though we have lost much of it at present, a few kind words would recover it all.

But if the tendency of this bill is, as I own it appears to me, to acquire a power of governing them by influence and corruption, in the first place, my Lords, this is not true government, but a sophisticated kind, which counterfeits the appearance, but without the spirit or virtue of the true: and then, as it tends to debase their spirits and corrupt their manners, to destroy all that is great and respectable in so considerable a part of the human species, and by degrees to gather them together with

the

the rest of the world, under the yoke of universal slavery; I think, for these reasons, it is the duty of every wise man, of every honest man, and of every Englishman, by all lawful means, to oppose it.

A

SPEECH, &c.

ON

THE APPEAL FROM A DECREE IN THE COURT OF CHANCERY,

IN FAVOR OF

LITERARY PROPERTY,

In the YEAR 1774.

# A SPEECH

ON

## LITERARY PROPERTY,

In the YEAR, 1774.

---

I BELIEVE, I shall have a great majority of the House with me, when I say, that in the course of this trial, we have heard enough to inform, and enough to puzzle us, it is this latter circumstance, that induces me to explain my own thoughts, before the most respectable of all audiences, not that I have the presumption, to think, I can say any thing that may deserve the least attention from

the

the great law Lords, but to others, whose understandings are of the same moderate size with my own, perhaps it may be of some use to explain my own difficulties, and my method of getting rid of them.

It seems to be acknowledged on all hands that this literary property did not exist before the invention of printing, and I will add, not for a considerable time after For, as every one had the liberty of copying whatever had been published before, and as printing is only a more expeditious method of copying, it necessarily follows that he who invented the art of printing, as long as he kept it to himself, must entirely monopolize that species of copying.

Authors, in this situation, were forced to make interest with printers to have their works printed; and even paid a sort of copy-money to the printers for doing them that honour. And this was, at that time,
a greater

a greater favour than we may possibly apprehend. For the first printers were authors themselves, and, you may depend upon it, always gave the preference to their own works. After this, princes assumed the sole controul of the press. They gave licences and privileges for what and to whom they pleased. They did, in all respects, what they pleased with books; and some of them were so unwise even as to write them. During all this time there is no appearance of a literary property vested in authors, and the possession of it at least seems to have been divided between the church, the state, and the stationers company. Yet, even at this time, there is supposed to have existed a copy-right, derived either from prerogative, from decrees of the star-chamber, from the stationers company, or from the law of nature. Now, my Lords, I own I distrust all

all these sources of common law we have been referred to except the last, I cannot argue from them, they do not convince me. I even think I can discover evident marks of sophistry and false reasoning.

But, my Lords, there is one source of law which has been very sparingly touched upon either by the able counsel, or by the learned judges, but which appears to me in dignity and authority far superior to any other we have heard of, and which yet is clear and intelligible even to us lay-lords; for in this case I have the honour to rank in that class myself; the source I am speaking of, is no other than that well-known and yet too much neglected source of public utility. Lawyers may have other ideas in their heads, but I am sure legislators ought to be governed by this. Through whatever channels law may flow in its progress, whether through the ada-

mantine

mantine fetters of prerogative, or the practice of courts, or the opinions of the sages of the law, or the bye-paths of the stationers company; it ought always to keep a fixed eye upon the public good. Even that pure fountain of immemorial custom, which is supposed to convey to us the wisdom of ages, and which certainly does not apply to the present case; even this first and most respectable source of law, is only valuable as it is presumed, by long trial and experience, to answer more surely the purposes of public good. Here we have a sure guide to follow, one that cannot lead us astray. Let us observe the straight, the plain, but the too little frequented path of public good, and if we make no considerable progress, we cannot err.

It is impossible, my Lords, for us to trace the progress of a law from its beginning;

ning, the history of it depends upon a sort of criticism that lies out of our way; but we may venture to pursue it in its consequences, and to judge of the cause by the effects. Let us consider the supposed common law before us by these rules.

By the statute law at present, authors are entitled to the exclusive privilege of printing their works for the term of fourteen years, which they have a power of renewing for fourteen years more. Besides this, there is claimed for them, for they claim nothing for themselves, an exclusive right of printing them for ever. Now it comes before us whether this last claim is founded in common law, and the safest and most practicable way of deciding the difficulty, is to enquire whether it is of public advantage to have it so, or if it may seem, perhaps, too much for us to to determine, in all cases, what is of pub-

lic

lic advantage, we may at least be confident that what is of evident public detriment is not the genuine produce of that wisdom of the nation, which is held forth to us by the common law.

In the first place, my Lords, I think it clear that this extension of the copy-right from twenty-eight years to all eternity, is no real benefit to authors themselves. For whatever pleasing dreams an author may form to himself of the life to come in every poet's creed, no bookseller will treat with him upon that footing. He will tell him that the market is glutted; that gentlemen and ladies have very little time for reading, and that it will be a long time before he shall be able to get off one impression. In short he will not suppose it possible that the work should last above five or six years, and will talk of seven as extreme old age for a modern performance. Authors

thors must necessarily come to the bookfellers terms till they grow rich men; or what is not much to be apprehended, till rich men turn authors. But 'in all cases that we have hitherto known, the author's interest is determined before the first fourteen years are expired, and, commonly, a long part of the term itself, and the whole immortality in reversion, must turn entirely to the profit of the bookseller. All the wisdom of the common law, in this instance, must of necessity deposit the whole profits of literature upon the booksellers. Under this law, in a certain length of time, these gentlemen will of course acquire a monopoly in all those valuable writings of their countrymen whose merit has made them survive the rest.

Now, my Lords, monopolies in general are odious. Good governments have sometimes favoured them for a short term, but I be-

I believe the most arbitrary government was never so unwise as to give a perpetual monopoly of any kind to one man and his heirs. But to vest in one particular set of men an hereditary and indefeasible monopoly in all the works of genius and literature, in the books of morals, science, and religion; in all useful and elegant compositions; this, my Lords, could not be the work of law or of nature; or it must be a strange *lusus naturæ*, the wildest prank that nature ever played. This is not the genuine offspring of that good old common law which, with infinite judgment and gravity, has accommodated itself to the great changes in human affairs, and has always kept her eye fixed upon the public good. It is a new spurious kind of macaroni common law, crept of late years into Westminster-hall, which dislikes the old-fashioned cut of our good old English rights and liberties; which endeavoured to prune and trim the rights of juries, and the liberty of the press, to the true foreign French fashion. This time two years it endeavoured to alter the laws of entail, and to give a stability to the property of a thimble or a nutmeg-grater, which the law does not give to our old demesne lands.

Let us but remove from our minds all this law juggling, all these indecent attempts to mislead us, by arguing from principles which we cannot understand, and there will not be the least difficulty in the present case. If this law is established, the booksellers will have the universal monopoly of knowledge we are speaking of. What use they will infallibly make of it, we may judge pretty tolerably from what they have done already. For many years backwards, they have partly
exercised

exercised the right which they now claim by law. What by collusive agreement among themselves; by bribing, and even pensioning some who opposed their claims; by intimidating the poorer sort, by using all arts to support their claim, and by watching a favourable current of opinion in Westminster Hall, they have, at last, obtained a verdict in their favour strengthened by a decree in the Court of Chancery. But, during all the time that this right has been only exercised by them, but not acknowledged, I appeal to your Lordships, whether the good standard books have not been printed as you would expect from monopolizers; the price raised; the paper, the print, and the binding growing daily worse. Have not the common editions of Milton, of the Spectator, of the other English books of great popular demand, been so printed as to make it evident that the sole end of the publisher was to get money, and not credit. I will venture to affirm, that the best books, and of the surest sale, have been always the worst printed. But more than this, they have sometimes refused to insert very considerable and useful improvements, when the work has a certain sale. A Right Reverend Prelate, who had very carefully collated the best editions of Locke's Essay on the Human Understanding, offered his notes and observations to a bookseller, who was publishing that work, he desired to be excused from printing them, alledging, that the work sold very well already.

And thus probably many useful additions may have been suppressed for fear of hurting the sale of old impressions, just as the fishmongers are said to destroy great quantities

ties of fish, for fear of over-stocking the market.

Another contrivance is, to vend a great deal of trash, under the credit of a few excellent pieces. Thus they will never print Addison's works, except in an expensive quarto edition, lest they should hurt the sale of the Spectators, Guardians, and Tatlers. Buxton waters, my Lords, are deservedly famous. The landlord, who has an exclusive right to the well, and the lodgings, gives worse fare and worse accommodation, than so much good company would meet with in any part of England. And if, after the cause before us is decided, which God forbid, in their favour, you want a Locke, or a Milton, from the only booksellers who will have the power to sell them; you must content yourself, at their own price, to take such paper, print, and binding as they shall think fit to give you. My Lords, it is a fact I have frequently heard mentioned, that, by lowering the price of ink, the bookfellers have obliged the makers to hurt and debafe the quality of it: fo that none of the books, which are now printed, are fit to be bound till they have lain by a year, and fome not even then. This, my Lords, is evident at firft fight. The printing ink is not black, it is a kind of a dull blueifh colour, with rather more of a dirty caft, but fomething like what the ladies call *petit gris*. For this reafon, Bafkerville, before he could make ufe of his elegant types, was obliged to manufacture his own ink. But if you have a mind to pafs a fair judgment on the effects of a monopoly on printing, allow me to mention the Bibles and Common Prayer Books, which are publifhed under a royal patent, and which, I believe, I may fay

without

without fear of being contradicted, were for a long time the very worst printed books in Europe. Could his Majesty, who is so generous a patron of liberal arts, have possibly by any human means been informed that an art, so deserving of royal encouragement, as that of printing, has been exercised ever since the revolution, to no other visible purpose but to blind and puzzle the best of his Majesty's subjects, and to make large dividends to the patentees, sure nothing would ever prevail upon him to renew so preposterous a grant The Roman Catholicks, for fear of making their common people too wise, have printed their Bible in an unknown tongue. It would have answered their purpose more decently, and almost as effectually, to have employed such printers as ours, for it signifies little, whether they have Bibles which they cannot understand,

derstand, or Bibles which they cannot read. I remember when Bibles and Common Prayer Books, that were printed at Edinburgh, bore an extravagant price because they were a little more legible than our own. That this disgraceful state of printing is owing entirely to the monopoly, may appear from hence, that in foreign Protestant countries, where the press is open, the Bibles and publick prayers are printed with clear and elegant types, superior in general to other Books in the language, not blotted and blurred, like our own, where the letters seem struggling to get from one side of the leaf to the other, and sometimes they succeed, sometimes meet half way, and cause a confusion which no eye can decypher. In order to convey the justest idea I can of the whole matter, allow me to tell a short story, and I hope I may claim your indulgence

gence for departing a very little from the gravity of my character. A stationer, in hopes of making his fortune, carried with him a large assortment of his own wares, and, amongst the rest, a great many of these Bibles we have been describing, and a large quantity of cards, and settled in North America. The cards sold amazingly; but the Bibles, being not quite so legible as the cards, stuck on his hands; to remedy this, he declared he would sell no more cards, unless they would consent to take a Bible with every pack. They demurred at first, but cards were to be had no where else, and the elderly ladies could not hold out, so he soon disposed of his Bibles.

This stationer, my Lords, was an extraordinary man. He is the first that has found out a method of levying an internal tax upon North America.

It appears to me, my Lords, extremely probable, that if we confirm this monopoly of the bookfellers, the fame game will be played in a different manner upon ourfelves. Thofe gentlemen, who by giving, 100 years ago, the 500th part of their value for the exclufive and everlafting property in the works of Locke and Milton, have purchafed a common law right to cheat us to what extent they pleafe, and may think it very reafonable not to part with one of thofe precious volumes, unlefs we chufe to take a bottle of Maredant's Drops, or of Beaume de Vie, with them. I fhall not be able to buy a volume of Tillotfon's Sermons, without having a gallipot of fomething or other tacked to them. This, perhaps, may be confidered as mere invention; but I have a right to fuggeft any poffible method that may be ufed by thofe who have a legal right

right to impose upon us, and, take my word for it, their invention is much better than mine. They are plodding men, who will think deeply on the subject, and make themselves masters of it.

But, my Lords, there are greater mischiefs remaining than any I have mentioned. If we are forced to pay a double price for our reading, to the greatest part of us it may be a very supportable tax; though even that may fall very heavy on men of real learning and genius in narrow circumstances. But, my Lords, this spirit of monopoly has a tendency to obstruct the advancement of knowledge. When Dr Smith, the late Master of Trinity College, was publishing his valuable Treatise of Optics, it became necessary, in the course of his work, to make long quotations from Sir Isaac Newton's Theory of Light and Colours. The bookseller, who
had

had the copy-right of that work (does it not hurt you, my Lords, to think that Sir Isaac Newton, the glory not of his country only, but of his age and species, who, certainly, if any author ever did write for mankind, and for immortality, it was him, should be the property of an imposing bookseller?) this proprietor of Sir Isaac Newton, insisted on his copy-right, and refused to let the Doctor print such long quotations without a valuable consideration. How the dispute ended, I cannot tell, but I know that it gave much plague to the author, and delayed his publication for a considerable time.

A very respectable Judge, to whom this country is obliged for a most excellent institute of laws, I am told has lately parted with the fee-simple of his works to a bookseller. The bookseller has since printed an octavo edition, with many large and

and important alterations; and has not, as in equity and gratitude he ought to have done, reprinted the alterations in the quarto fize, for the benefit of fuch of his readers as have bought the large edition. Does not this proceeding amount to a declaration, that the faid bookfeller is determined, by every way he can think of, to impofe upon the public, to the utmoft of his poor abilities. To perfift in exercifing the abufes of thofe rights, at the very time they are called in queftion, fhows a moft incurable habit of impofition.

I have only mentioned a few cafes that I have either been acquainted with myfelf, or have lately met with in converfation, and fhall tire your Lordfhips with no more. Only permit me to remind you that one of the learned Judges complained of the enormous dearnefs of law-books, which, as it was contradicted by no one prefent, I think

think we may confider as a point determined by all the twelve Judges.

It has been obferved, and it is a pleafure to hear it from the learned Judges, that, by the common law, every right has a remedy; and I hope that, by the common law, every wrong has a remedy too. Now, my Lords, I fhould be glad to know what remedy there is for the wrongs which are every day fuftained by his Majefty's fubjects from the bookfellers, and whether, if the common law is, in itfelf, fo wife and fagacious as Lord Coke reprefents it to be, it would not rather have chofen to reftrain their depredations, than to enlarge their privileges.

My Lords, there is another difadvantage arifing from this monopoly, of a national kind, that deferves your ferious attention. Whilft thefe gentlemen are intent on the advantages of their copy-rights, and being

fure

sure of a sale, consider only the cheapness, and not the excellence, of the work, every material of the manufacture, is debased; the workmen become mere drudges, without spirit or emulation; and no work is undertaken that is to do honour to the press, and depend upon the workmanship for sale, the classics, and other books that are open to all, will be printed at Glasgow and Edinburgh, or imported from Holland. I am told, that in London, they have almost forgot the art of printing Latin and Greek; and that Mr. Bowyer, who is very superior to his profession, is the only man at present qualified to be the editor of a work of learning.

Now, my Lords, allow me to hope, that our votes shall this day set at liberty the spirit, the activity, and the inventive genius of our countrymen, that have been cramped and fettered too long by this monopoly.

nopoly. Why may not the English printers attain to that respectable pre-eminence which our artificers of other kinds have acquired over the workmen of other nations? In every part of Europe our language is studied, and there is a demand for our authors. If these are well printed, they will be purchased every where with greediness, and why may we not, in a short time, by the talent of improvement which is natural to us, be able to supply other nations with more elegant editions of the Greek and Latin writers, and of the best French and Italian books, than they have yet seen; which, at the same time that they do honour to our press, may procure a beneficial commerce to our country.

I would not be understood, by any thing I have said of booksellers, to represent them as a worse sort of men than their neighbours. The law which puts it in their power,

power, and makes it their intereſt, to defraud us, makes them by degrees, conſider thoſe frauds as innocent. What happens in the common courſe of buſineſs, is always held excuſable But, my Lords, in a ſerious light, I think it a very powerful additional objection againſt this copy-right, that it tends to corrupt the natural honeſty and integrity of thoſe who are poſſeſſors of it.

Now, putting all theſe circumſtances together which I have been able to touch upon, but very ſuperficially, the ſordid and unlimited impoſitions of bookſellers, the obſtructions laid in the paths of knowledge; and the total deſtruction of a very honourable branch of commerce, all that we have ſuffered, and all that we have loſt, and all that we are likely to ſuffer and loſe by this propoſed extenſion of their privileges; let me aſk your Lordſhips with the utmost seriousness and candor, whether it is possible that a genuine branch of the common law should necessarily lead us into so many mischiefs and inconveniences? In mathematical reasonings, we often come designedly to a false conclusion, in order to show the falsehood of the principles we reasoned upon. In enquiries concerning law and morals, if we are led to some proposition that is hurtful and pernicious to society, we are equally sure that the principles we went upon are unsound. Now, since this monopoly of booksellers has appeared, upon examination, to be a certain source and a constant encouragement of impositions, frauds, and knavery, and a restraint upon learning and commerce, I think myself authorised to infer, with the utmost certainty, that the literary property, from which it necessarily proceeds, is not a genuine produce of the common law,

but

but a mere fiction and imposture. I am sure of the imposture itself, though I may not be able to trace it to its source, or to follow it through all its appearances.

My Lords, if the decree before us should be affirmed, it will be a sort of misfortune to us to have had such men as Locke and Newton for our countrymen. The rest of the world will have the liberty of reading their works, published with all the advantages arising from freedom and emulation. To us they will be doled out like some quack medicine, at what price, and under what conditions the bookseller shall think fit to impose. The writings of these great men, my Lords, are the property, as well as the glory, of the country.

Let me add but one short argument more, but which, in my opinion, is decisive. If this literary property had been established beyond all possibility of contradiction at common law, if it was supported by immemorial custom, by the uniform opinions of great lawyers, and a long series of adjudged cases, I should acknowledge it with great reluctance, and should be puzzled with it as with some strange preternatural produce of the common law, but should think it highly necessary for the legislature to interpose, and to limit by statute a perpetual right, that must otherwise be the source of great inconvenience and great injustice.

But when, in support of this right, we meet with no opinions of learned lawyers, no adjudged cases, except such as are not applicable, or not competent to the present case, but certainly not conclusive, when the grounds on which it is built are metaphysical arguments and subtle distinctions, never used before, and invented only for the present occasion, I cannot but think

think we are at liberty to govern our judgments by the great mafter principle of all law, the good of the public; which is not fond of temporary monopolies, but cannot endure a perpetual one. We can certainly do no great harm upon this occafion, by paying a little attention to the Public Good.

A

SPEECH, &c. &c.

ON THE

BILL

FOR REPEALING

THE PENAL LAWS

AGAINST

PROTESTANT DISSENTERS,

In the Year 1779.

# A
# SPEECH,
### &c. &c. &c.

---

I RISE up, my Lords, not from the vanity of a speaker, which, God knows, I have no pretensions to, but I feel myself under a strong obligation to give some reasons for my opinion, in a case where I stand almost single from my brethren.

In the first place, I give my consent
most

most fully and sincerely to the Bill as it now stands, repealing all the penal laws against the Protestant Dissenters. These laws were, from the beginning, the disgrace of the national church.

They were passed originally from no publick-spirited, and from no truly religious motive. They were the produce of revenge, of a spirit of party and persecution, inconsistent with our national liberty, and our national character. To the repeal of these laws I consent most cordially, and, if the Bill is confined to that single point, I shall look upon it as the best proof of political wisdom that I have ever been witness to within these walls. But the additional clause, imposing a confession of faith upon them (short and general, and true, as it undoubtedly is), has a very different complexion from the rest. I
hope

hope it will be underſtood that a Proteſtant Biſhop can have no poſſible objection to the declaring in his own perſon, that the Scriptures contain the revealed will of God, and are the rule of his faith and practice. This is evidently the moſt fundamental article of our religion; every other article depends upon the truth of it. I not only believe it, but hope I ſhould have the virtue, if called upon, to ſeal it with my blood. And yet, my Lords, the moſt ſacred truth I believe myſelf, I do not think that I have any right to impoſe upon other men. Only let it be remembered, that I acknowledge the truth of the declaration, and object ſolely to the impoſition of it.

For let me obſerve, in the firſt place, that, by adding this clauſe, we convert the Bill, from being a repeal of all former penal laws, into a penal law itſelf, for
thoſe

those who do not subscribe the declaration, remain still liable to all the old penalties.

But why is this declaration necessary to be imposed? Is there a Protestant congregation in this kingdom, is there one in all Europe, which does not believe that the Scriptures are the revealed will of God, and the rule of faith and practice? The publick worship, at least the greatest part of it, every where consists in reading and explaining the Holy Scriptures. The Bible is the acknowledged religion of every Protestant congregation. Whoever receives the Scriptures at all, receives them as the will of God. Take away the authority of the Holy Scriptures, and all Protestant congregations are dissolved at once. If all we want is to have this truth admitted by all Protestant congregations, we may be satisfied to our hearts content, for there never yet existed a single Protestant

testant who denied it; and I will venture to prophefy there never will

But fuppofe there was fomewhere a fet of Chriftians, who did not receive our Canon of Scripture; fuppofe they built their faith upon fome of the old fpurious Gofpels, or fuppofe that they rejected fome of our canonical books; or fuppofe that they rejected all infpired writings, and placed their faith only on the fecret influences of the Spirit. Would you perfecute them for believing the Chriftian Religion, on arguments that fuit their own underftanding? The queftion is not whether they judge wrong, but whether they are not to be tolerated, although they judge wrong We all allow, in every one of the fuppofitions we have made, that the Diffenters would be in error, but errors in matters of Religion are the very ground and fubject of Toleration.

I wifh,

I wish, too, your Lordships would consider who are the men that would be the greatest sufferers by this imposition. The most conscientious, the most learned, and the most respectable of the Dissenting Ministers. A great majority of these, I am told, declare against all human authority in matters of Religion. They hold that no church has a right to impose an article of faith on any other religious community. I believe from my heart that they say true; at least, if they do not, he that can confute them is a much abler man than myself. Now, my Lords, these are men, who deserve our esteem for their science, their literature, their critical study of the Scriptures, and their excellent writings either defending or teaching common Christianity; and, my Lords, they have of late stood forth almost singly in defence of the natural, civil, and religious rights of mankind.

mankind. I will presume to say it will be no disparagement to this bench to consider such men as our friends and brethren, not as odious rivals, that want to scramble with us for perferment and power; but as fellow-labourers, engaged in the same honorable task with ourselves, to instruct mankind in the art of true happiness. And I respect them the more for having gone such lengths in learning and enquiry, when the utmost reward of their ambition can very little exceed £100 *per ann.* Yet, my Lords, if we enact this clause, and put it in execution, these men will not even be tolerated.

My Lords, I can hardly venture to pronounce what sort of conduct and sentiment is suitable to our present state of humiliation.

Let me recall your thoughts to that state of imperial greatness and dignity, which

which we were possessed of, before the Ministry had persuaded you to vote it away. America was filled with every different sect, that was the growth of this country and their own; besides some that were imported from Germany. All of them were tolerated, they were used to see their neighbours enjoy the divine worship they liked best, and were happy in possessing the same privileges themselves; in consequence of this, all has been peace and harmony. No religious differences have given the least disturbance to Government for the last century.

We were, indeed, disappointed in our hopes of establishing episcopacy in America. But, even that point, if I am rightly informed, might have been carried, had it not been for the total supineness and negligence of the Ministers; who have never cared

cared for any thing belonging to bishops, but their votes.

Look upon the state of Bengal, where every sect, and every superstition, from the days of Zoroaster, to the present age; from the worshippers of fire and idols, down to the disciples of Mahomet, are tolerated. No government has ever made more free with the property of their subjects, than our countrymen there have done, yet, even they have left the poor Gentoos their religion, who have left them nothing else: but, I will venture to say, that even that poor, passive, effeminate race, could not have been governed without a general toleration; without this general toleration, the immense empire we are now losing, would have been lost long before.

The whole subject of toleration, is not properly a question relating to the church, but the state. And allow me to say, with all due respect to this Right Reverend Bench, that we ourselves are not the very men, to whose decision I would chuse to commit it. It is the duty of the magistrate (for it is the very end of magistracy) to protect all men in the enjoyment of their natural rights, and allow me to consider the free exercise of our religion, as one of the first and best of them.

Consider what has been the practice of the wisest and freest states. All nations have been favorable to toleration, in proportion to their improvements, and their freedom. The Dutch at first made trial of persecution, like their neighbours; but, they soon found that sober and industrious subjects were worth preserving, whether they were Jews, Turks, Infidels, or Heretics.

It is a singular observation, and which I think should have the greatest weight with a legislature, that though all modern history is full of mischiefs, occasioned by the want of toleration; yet, no author has ever undertaken to shew, that any public evils have any where been occasioned by toleration.

And though toleration is the natural growth of only free Governments; yet the disadvantages of an intolerant spirit are so great, and so apparent, that arbitrary states have been forced, out of mere selfish prudence, to defeat their own principles, and to tolerate the heretic, in order to preserve the manufacturer. France has thought it prudent, to connive at the religion of the Protestants, in consideration of their usefulness and industry.

Here, my Lords, I feel it necessary to take some notice of the petition from the

University of Oxford, out of the respect I bear, and the relation I have formerly held to that seat of learning.

It is there apprehended, that if persons are suffered to teach as Dissenting Ministers, without making any declaration, that even Atheists might be admitted, and men who would teach any doctrines contrary to the principles of Christianity. In the first place, allow me to observe, that the apprehensions of these learned gentlemen are contrary to plain experience We have lived the best part of a century, without enforcing the declarations or subscriptions, that are enjoined by law. To all practical purposes, they have had no existence any where, but in the statute book. Now, let me ask, whether any such consequences have appeared? Have those, who are called Protestant Dissenters, held any doctrines incompatible with the principles

ciples of Christianity and the good of society? Have they not been considered in the two former reigns as loyal subjects, and as good citizens? Can Oxford herself boast of having produced more steady friends to the House of Hanover?

But, in truth, my Lords, the Lay Protestant Dissenters would no more bear to be taught such impious doctrines, than the Universities themselves. No sect ever consisted of hypocrites. The majority, in their religious enquiries, seek after truth and happiness, and are sometimes apt too easily to believe they have found them. If I may speak from the information of a very narrow and accidental acquaintance, I must say they have laymen amongst them of liberal education, and who have exercised their understandings with as much freedom, care, and ability, as any men I have known of our own church. Men of this character will have weight wherever they are, and they will neither admit themselves, nor suffer their neighbours to admit, such teachers into their pulpits as the Oxford gentlemen are alarmed at.

The most pernicious principles to society, and the most repugnant to the true spirit of Christianity, that ever obtained a firm footing in this country, are the old Tory principles. The Dissenters are, at least, clear and innocent of this guilt. These principles, of late, have been carefully nursed and revived. They have almost ventured to appear at Court, but have shewn themselves, without disguise, in the ministerial writers. Let it be allowed me, with the most respectful tenderness, to admonish that learned body, to whom I owed the pleasures of my youth, and that foundation of science and useful literature, which I have since too little cul-

cultivated,—let me conjure them not to suffer those odious principles to revive again within their walls, which are as incompatible with true learning as they are with liberty. The men who have given up their love of freedom, and have forgot the natural rights of mankind, have lost the best and most vital part—of the vigour and nerves of their understanding. They are neither able to discover truth, nor to relish science. No Jacobite was ever a philosopher.

But to pretend to support the House of Hanover by those stale and impotent principles, which ruined the House of Stuart, is a greater degree of sophistry and nonsense than has ever yet appeared in the Schools. Suppose it possible, that the people of England should so far lose their senses, as generally to adopt the old Tory principles, how soon might they be turned

this character will have weight wherever they are, and they will neither admit themselves, nor suffer their neighbours to admit, such teachers into their pulpits as the Oxford gentlemen are alarmed at.

The most pernicious principles to society, and the most repugnant to the true spirit of Christianity, that ever obtained a firm footing in this country, are the old Tory principles. The Dissenters are, at least, clear and innocent of this guilt. These principles, of late, have been carefully nursed and revived. They have almost ventured to appear at Court, but have shewn themselves, without disguise, in the ministerial writers. Let it be allowed me, with the most respectful tenderness, to admonish that learned body, to whom I owed the pleasures of my youth, and that foundation of science and useful literature, which I have since too little cul-

cultivated,—let me conjure them not to suffer those odious principles to revive again within their walls, which are as incompatible with true learning as they are with liberty. The men who have given up their love of freedom, and have forgot the natural rights of mankind, have lost the best and most vital part—of the vigour and nerves of their understanding. They are neither able to discover truth, nor to relish science. No Jacobite was ever a philosopher.

But to pretend to support the House of Hanover by those stale and impotent principles, which ruined the House of Stuart, is a greater degree of sophistry and nonsense than has ever yet appeared in the Schools. Suppose it possible, that the people of England should so far lose their senses, as generally to adopt the old Tory principles, how soon might they be turned against the Administration that labours to propagate them! How soon might our inveterate enemies, whom the blunders of our Ministers have united and made powerful, introduce a competitor for the Crown, who has an older and a better title to the benefit of those principles!—Instead of this mean, dishonest, view, let them instil into the noble youth committed to their care, a thirst of knowledge, a taste for science, a warm love of liberty, virtue, and their country. Let them instruct them in the true constitution of government, not in the old system of bondage and servility, but in that great reformation of government which was brought about by King William, the spirit and the memory of which are almost lost, together with the greatness and glory that were the fruit of it.

In this country, my Lords, religious and

and party zeal has passed many severe laws against Dissenters, and, for many years, the State has had the wisdom not to execute them.

Even this clause, which I object to, when it was asked at a meeting of the Right Reverend Bench, where I had the honour to be present, whether it was ever intended to be put in execution? It was answered, NO, there was no such intention. I asked then, and I ask now, What was the use of making laws that were never to be executed? It was said, to be suitable to our dignity and our authority.

To make good and useful laws, such as carry in them their own force and evidence, is a work of great dignity and authority; but to make useless and insignificant laws, is not to exercise authority, but to lessen and degrade it. It is a vain, idle, and insolent parade of legislation;
tending

tending only to show that we know not how to use the powers we are trusted with.

And yet, my Lords, would to God, the four last shameful and miserable years had been employed only in making such trifling laws as these. This wretched country might still have been safe, and perhaps, once more, might have been happy; and Government would only have lost, what it never seems to have cared for, a little more of its dignity and credit.

And let us for one moment consider in what hands is to be lodged this power of regulating religious doctrines, and prescribing articles of faith. Certainly, in this country, we must place this holy deposit where we have placed every thing else that is great and good; the honour, the interest, and the revenues of our country; our hopes, our public confidence, and the majority

majority of our votes; all must undoubtedly be placed in the keeping of the Ministry.

Now, my Lords, this system of church government would, in my opinion, be the most effectual method we could take to increase the body of the Dissenters. Some very good Christians of our own church, might possibly make a few reasonable objections to letting the Ministry for the time being, cut and shuffle their religion for them. And, perhaps, my Lords, there might be Ministers to whose management, none who have the least value for their religion would chuse to commit it. One might naturally ask a Minister for a good pension, or a good contract, or a place at Greenwich Hospital, but hardly any one would think of using their interest to get him a place in heaven. What I now say applies only to future bad Ministers, for, of the present Administration, I most firmly believe that they are full as capable of defining articles of faith, as of directing the counsels of state.

I shall end what I proposed to say, with observing, that the ruling party is always very liberal in bestowing the title of Schismatics and Heretics on those who differ from them in matters of religion, and representing them as dangerous to the state. My Lords, the contrary is the truth: those who are uppermost, and have the power, are the men who do the mischief; the Schismatics only suffer and complain, and are often thought worthy of punishment for that very reason. Ask who has brought the affairs of this country into the present calamitous state? Who are the men that have plundered and depopulated Bengal? Who are they that have turned a whole continent, inhabited by friends and kindred,

kindred, into our bittereft enemies? Yes! they who have fhorn the ftrength, and cut off the right arm of Britain were all members of the eftablifhed church, all orthodox men.—I am not afraid of thofe tender and fcrupulous confciences who are over cautious of profeffing or believing too much; if they are fincerely in the wrong, I forgive their errors, and refpect their integrity. The men I am afraid of, are the men who believe every thing, and fubfcribe every thing, and who vote for every thing.

# SERMON

PREACHED BEFORE

# THE HOUSE OF LORDS,

IN THE ABBEY CHURCH OF

## ST PETER, WESTMINSTER,

ON TUESDAY, JANUARY 30, 1770,

Being the Day appointed to be observed as the Day of the Martyrdom of King Charles I.

# SERMON

PREACHED BEFORE THE

# HOUSE OF LORDS.

---

Isa xxxiii. part of ver. 6.

*And wisdom and knowledge shall be the stability of thy times.*

As the form of this world, and of the most considerable objects in it, is continually varying; and, as things acquire and lose importance by the changes of time and circumstances, I hope I shall not be thought to have departed too far from the limits prescribed to me, if I consider my subject in the point of view, which seems most to merit your attention at present, and is most likely to suggest the means and excite the desire of serving our country. To this end, I shall take leave to regard the guilty scenes we commemorate, not as the whole of my subject, but as one link of that long chain of causes, which the wisdom of Providence has been employing, for the space of several ages, in forming the manners and character of this distinguished nation. The doctrine contained in my text, and implying that improvements in knowledge and arts, add not only to the credit, but to the strength and security of a nation, will be better illustrated by this manner of treating my subject, than from a regular comment on the words themselves. " And wisdom and " knowledge shall be the stability of thy " times."

This country has not always enjoyed that pre-eminence of power and dignity which

which it is now possessed of. Before the Reformation, our ancestors had shown themselves capable of war and conquests; had given proofs of manly sense, and a spirit of freedom in the frame of their laws and constitution; and had produced some rare examples of learning and genius: but, upon the whole, they must be acknowledged to have been very inferior to the southern parts of Europe in literature, in manners, in commerce, and in the arts of life. It must be owned too, that the attention of our countrymen was awakened by slow degrees, and not till most other parts of Europe had been struck with the novelty, the truth, and the great importance of the doctrine taught by the Reformers. They were then little versed in the arts of controversy; and the part they took, was more owing to the example of their neighbours, and to the influence of political events, than to the love of truth and the spirit of inquiry. But they soon began to feel and exercise their own powers, and growing interested in so important a cause, they proceeded at length in the work of reformation with as much learning and sagacity, and more good sense and moderation, than the ablest of their teachers And though the good work was soon interrupted by the revival of popery, yet the short continuance, and the violent effects of it, excited a warmer zeal for reformation, and gave strength and spirit to their after-endeavours. It was long before the fear of popery subsided, and while it lasted, it encouraged a careful study of the Scriptures, and a critical examination of the grounds on which its principal doctrines were founded. And the new sects that started up continually, by furnishing fresh matter of dispute, en-

larged

larged the bounds of inquiry, and accustomed men to defend themselves against attacks from every quarter.

The mind of man easily proceeds from one discovery to others of a similar kind. It was natural for them, who had just freed themselves from the encroachments of ecclesiastical power, to enquire into the rights and authority of civil government. Even under the prosperous reign of Elizabeth, there appeared a disposition to examine into the grounds and foundations of those powers which were exercised with moderation, glory and utility. Instead of allaying this inquisitive spirit, her successor acted as if it had been policy to encourage it. His feeble acts of violence, and the declamations he wrote, to convince his people of the excellence of arbitrary government, could only tend to excite those jealousies, and stir those questions, which a wife prince would chuse to suppress. For it is the wisdom of government to prevent enquiries into the origin of its powers, by answering the good purposes for which they were granted or assumed.

In the unfortunate days that followed, the spirit of enquiry, that had been raised, became more vehement and more general. Their religious and civil disputes were blended together, and communicated their rage and acrimony to each other. On one side, the necessary acts of authority were considered as oppression, and on the other, the just remonstrances of the people were treated as sedition. This irritable state of mind is certainly not the most favourable for the discovery of truth; but yet it may help to shake off prejudices, and prepare the understanding to make a proper use of the calm, that follows such agitations.

For

For in those days, the reverence that had been annexed to old opinions, was shaken and impaired by the violent attacks that were made upon them. The received dictates of law and government were confuted by the sense of oppression, and the impulse of necessity. Their grievances were heavy and palpable. The hand of violence hung over their heads, and their terrors were awakened by their sufferings. It was not then necessary to convince them of their dangers by long and intricate reasonings; or to use persuasion and intreaties, to make them sensible of their grievances. They acted in consequence of their feelings, and burst the chains of sophistry and violence, by the efforts which sense and nature made to preserve themselves. We ought to think over the transactions of those times with tenderness, for they were the actions of our forefathers: not to engage in their paffions, but to draw with temper and mildnefs, fuch admonitions from their hiftory, as may teach us to avoid civil diffentions, and to value peace and good government, to confider the outrages of the times, the public miferies, the fatal end of a mifguided virtuous prince, and the ftate of horror and confufion they lived in, as one of the great fcenes which Providence fometimes introduces to execute its myfterious purpofes; and which, at that time, produced a vifible change in the manners and opinions of the nation. For, in that fierce conflict of tempers, interefts, and characters, of enthufiafm and fuperftition; of tyranny and faction, of ambition and liberty; of all the vices and virtues exerted with as much force and induftry as human nature could employ; great and valuable talents were formed, beneficial views were opened, and the

outlines

outlines of many important truths were struck out with incorrect boldness and strength. And though the majority of all parties were too much prejudiced, and too much heated to see truth in any sect but their own, yet there were a few, who were able to possess their faculties, and to look with temper on the confusion and madness of the times. To them, the distresses of their country, amidst scenes of horror and melancholy, afforded much matter for reflection, and many inlets of improvement. They were taught to distinguish the true boundaries of reason and religion, by the strange deviations from them that were before their eyes: they saw the excesses of liberty, and the evils of tyranny and oppression, and that both are equally inconsistent with the rights and the happiness of mankind: and they learned from the irreconcilable variety

variety of opinions, that toleration and mutual indulgence are principles of natural juftice, and the only practicable conditions of living in peace and charity. Thefe were of that fort of men whofe talents give them an authority over the minds of others. They taught their countrymen to think and reafon with more clearnefs, and in a natural language, free from fcholaftic fubtleties and the affectation of learning, and to the honour of the eftablifhed church, the greateft part of them were her members. From hence we may conclude, that during the miferies of the civil wars; and perhaps through the experience of thofe miferies, under that all-wife direction which bringeth good out of evil, the nation in general was acquiring a more comprehenfive view of things, and jufter notions of religion and government.

In the times fucceeding the Reftoration, religion

religion and liberty had much to fear; but those times were not unfavourable to the improvement of knowledge. The rights of the people were left insecure and undetermined, and they were always in danger from the power, the claims, and the insidious arts of government, besides the remains of some old prejudices in favour of arbitrary principles. But then this situation obliged them to a stronger exertion of their faculties, made them vigilant and attentive; and gave constant exercise to their reason on the most important of all subjects, religion and government. In other great kingdoms, the liberty of enquiring into men's natural rights had been suppressed for the security of the state, in ours, the endeavour to suppress it gave warmth and spirit to the exercise of it. There were also other objects of importance, which at that time

claimed

claimed the attention of the people. Fresh matter was furnished to their enquiry and imitation, by the growth of manufactures, the extension of commerce, and the improvement of navigation; for in those great sources of national strength, some neighbouring states were still superior to us. It was also our good fortune to avail ourselves of the folly and cruelty of our neighbours, who drove into our arms some thousands of their most deserving subjects, and with them many useful arts and inventions; rather than they would permit them to worship the God of their fathers, after the manner which they called heresy. That all these causes of improvement were not without their effect, may be collected from the progress then made by some of our contemplative countrymen, in the most arduous of all sciences. For they were the inventors of that clear, simple, and sublime

lime philosophy, which remains to this day the noblest and most succesful effort of human genius, and which is still more valuable for its method and principles, than for its discoveries. Such exalted talents and abilites, so superior to the highest attainments of other men, could not have been formed amongst an ignorant people. It was in vain to expect that a nation possessed of these high endowments, and full of the conscious pride that accompanies them, should submit with patience to part with them, and whatever else they held dear, at the command of an arbitrary prince. Yet there was one found weak and unjust enough to require from them such a sacrifice. The event was, that his subjects saw, with a proper indignation, the mischief that was prepared for them, and wisely giving up, for a time, the views of their respective parties, the members

of

of the established church, and the Protestant Dissenters of all kinds, uniting their efforts, and joining in one great, durable, and national interest; they burst at once the chains of slavery and superstition, because it was not possible that they should be holden of them.

The conduct of our ancestors at this period, the courage and firmness with which they asserted their liberties, the temper and wisdom they discovered in the constitution of their government, and the tenderness and humanity with which they listened to the prejudices, and adjusted the claims of their fellow-citizens, afforded at that time a great and instructive spectacle to the rest of the world, and an example of right behaviour on signal trying occasions, which ought to be ever dear to their posterity.

And we ought to remember, with gratitude

tude and veneration, how much the nation was then indebted to that wife and fingular monarch; that hero without paffion or vanity, whofe virtues and fervices, we muft own, with fhame, were not sufficiently refpected by our anceftors.

From this æra we firft obtained a profpect of better times; an age of domeftic peace and liberty; of knowledge and arts; of private happinefs and publick glory. The improvement of commerce was the immediate confequence of freedom, to an active people, poffeffed of great natural advantages, and who had acquired the fkill to ufe them. And their endeavours were animated, and their views enlightened by their alliance and intercourfe with a wife commercial republic, which had firft taught the world, what great things may be effected by induftry, when protected by a free government. From that period,

period, notwithstanding the interested views of men in power, and the opposition which even their best intentions are sure to meet with from their competitors; notwithstanding the contradictory measures of parties, and the accidental madness of the populace; yet, upon the whole, the great objects of publick national good have been better understood, and more successfully cultivated, than in any other age. The people who had shown such activity and vigour in their former precarious state of liberty, did not slacken their endeavours, when the full and free exercise of their powers, and all the advantages arising from it were secured to them. It would be a task of more labour than use, to trace out the particular steps of their advancement in commerce and arts. Let those who have visited other countries, compare the most flourishing of them with the present fent ftate of their own; and let thofe who are advanced in years, call to mind the appearance of things which they faw in their childhood, and then, after furveying the face of this kingdom in town and country, the extenfion of agriculture, the new arts of cultivation, the works of publick utility, the rivers, the plantations, and the buildings, which caft a luftre over the whole ifland, add to this the neatnefs, convenience, and elegance, diffufed through the middle rank of life, and penetrating into the moft obfcure and diftant parts; and having furveyed all this, let them judge of the caufe by its effects, and eftimate the fpirit and underftanding of this nation, by the greatnefs and the rapidity of its improvements. That ufeful fpecies of philofophy which we mentioned above, which traces out the operations of nature by well-chofen experiments, and patient observation; which is the offspring of our own country, and which spreading from hence, has improved and enlightened great part of the world; has mixed its beneficial influence with the management of commerce, the cultivation of arts, and even with the common employments of life. The pursuit of natural knowledge still continues; not indeed with a success that equals the great discoveries made by our fathers, when the secrets of nature were first laid open to them: but yet the common stock is still increasing by daily additions, and there remain very valuable gleanings, after the full harvest of science, which they had the advantage of reaping before us. Every profession has shaken off its antient prejudices, and learned to reason and judge, in their respective provinces, with greater accuracy, and on better principles. The civil and religious disputes

disputes which exercised the passions of our forefathers, have lost their virulence, having at last undergone that cool examination, which always produces either unanimity or peace. The dissentions in state have not been kindled for many years by the fury of national parties, but by that ambition and struggle for power, which will ever be inseparable from human nature. If the passions of the people have sometimes been inflamed by the instigation of factious leaders, or by some unjustifiable steps of government; the storm has soon spent itself, and without any mischievous effects. Even the present distractions of the times, which have been owing to causes very disproportionable to their effects, and been fomented by the arts of men whose wisdom is certainly not equal to their ambition, will subside of themselves, as soon as the good sense of

the

the people has calmed their apprehensions. It will not long be practicable to keep alive groundless jealousies, and to alarm their minds with the dread of grievances which they neither feel nor understand: and our Sovereign, in due time, will reap the fruits of his patience and long-suffering, of his care for the happiness, and his indulgence for the errors of his people. All this, and greater things than these, may with assurance be hoped for from that solid and clear good sense, which has now been improving by the constant experience and discipline of several ages, and which may justly be considered as the characteristic of this nation, which, when unbiassed, and left to itself, has a wonderful discernment in the characters of men, is able to instruct statesmen and ministers in the great objects of public utility, and the means of attaining them; and when it acts with

with freedom, carries with it that invincible spirit, which can execute every practicable undertaking; which is itself the greatest of all our national resources; and will be found, in times of severe trial, capable of doing greater things for the public service, than experience has yet shown, or imagination suggested to us.

Let it be allowed me, on this occasion, to dwell only on the merits and improvements of my countrymen, in which they excel mankind, at least, to wish that it was excusable to pass over in silence the profligacy and licentiousness, the insatiable love of pleasure, the contempt of order and law, of religion and government, which have already prevailed too far, and which are the natural effects of great prosperity upon vulgar minds. And though the vast numbers who manage the business, and support the honour of the nation, cannot be deeply infected with these vices; and the instances we meet with in private life of every amiable and useful virtue, ought to be kept in our minds on this occasion, yet such is undeniably the growing corruption of our public manners, as ought to give a very just alarm, not only to the friends of religion, but to the lovers of their country. But let us hope, that the sense and virtue of this people will exert themselves to prevent their own destruction; let us hope more from that over-ruling Providence, which has always protected, and which has often saved us, and let us turn our eyes from this melancholy view of things, which neither our subject nor our inclination lead us to pursue.

The reflections which we have made in honour of our country (true and just as we esteem them) would be very unworthy of of this place and occasion, if they were to terminate in mere amusement, or in the indulgence of that vanity which all men assume to themselves from the exploits and renown of their countrymen. Yet, I hope, I shall be justified, when I remind you, that these reflections ought to be taken into consideration, when we endeavour to form a reasonable notion of that important moral duty, the love of our country. If the society we live in has really the superiority we boast of, over other communities, in wisdom, intelligence, the laws of government, and the arts of life, it certainly ought to be served, defended, and obeyed, with proportionable degrees of spirit and affection. The inhabitants of this country would ill deserve their wealth and plenty, all the advantages and ornaments of life, of which they have so large a share; the liberty they are proud of, and that pure religion which their fathers were ready to die for, and which they too much neglect, if they showed no more zeal for the government which procures them these advantages, than the oppressed subjects of some kingdoms do, for the laws and customs which are the causes of their misery. Our countrymen, on the contrary, have reasons of the most powerful kind to love a community, which is so eminently distinguished by its merits, its happiness, its beneficial views and purposes. It is honourable, it is virtuous to promote the interest of a community, which aims not at greatness by unjust measures, which seeks not conquest, and the means of tyrannizing over its neighbours, but rather to maintain equality and independence between bordering states, and to suppress the ambition of others; which founds all the superiority it pretends to,

on

on a more dextrous application of the gifts of nature to the purposes of life, and on communicating useful arts and inventions to the rest of the world. It is the common interest of mankind that a nation, to whom they are so much indebted, should be reverenced and supported, and enjoy its glories in a state of permanent prosperity. But they who are the subjects of such a government, ought to preserve a deep and lively sense of their own privileges and happiness, and to assume that virtuous pride which makes men worthy of the honours that are conferred on them. They should reverence a constitution, from which they have derived a long continuance of blessings, and they ought to study the principles, and consider the structure of it, that they may be qualified to preserve, to defend, and to improve it.

The warmest loyalty, and the most willing

ing obedience, is due to him who is intrusted with the execution of such a noble system of laws, for it is only in obedience to the laws, that the effect and excellence of government is seen. And as there is no other people, who so well knows the ends and the advantages of government, there is none who ought so cheerfully to submit to their governors. To scrutinize their conduct with rigour and malice, is unwise and ungenerous. It deprives them of their just and natural reward, the exquisite pleasure which is felt in serving a grateful people: it diverts them from the great objects of public good, and it discourages men of mild and ingenuous tempers from the service of their country. But it has always been the weakness of our countrymen, to exercise their discernment with too much severity on public affairs, and to require more at the hands

of

of their rulers, than can reasonably be expected from creatures like men. And yet, that their statesmen have not, in general, been so corrupt, or so incapable, as they seem to take for granted, may appear from this single consideration; that it is by a series of administrations, almost every one of which has been unpopular in its turn, that this kingdom has attained to its envied power and prosperity. And let us reflect with due candour, that it requires talents and experience of the most universal kind, to manage the affairs of a nation, whose commerce, empire, and influence, renders it more or less connected with every other people.

There are other reflections arising from the view we have taken of our subject, not unworthy the attention of statesmen and ministers.

To preside over a people which has so many

many titles of pre-eminence above other nations, is the higheſt office in value and dignity which can fall to the lot of man. It opens, to a generous mind, the nobleſt, the greateſt, the moſt practicable means of ſerving our country, and doing the moſt extenſive good to our fellow-creatures. Great part of the work is made eaſy to them by a conſtitution of government, and a ſyſtem of laws, which carry with them the experience and wiſdom of ages; ſuch as the moſt comprehenſive mind of itſelf could never have invented, and would chuſe to be reſtrained by, but, indeed, they are not properly reſtraints; but the rules which wiſdom and goodneſs have formed to themſelves, for the execution of their own purpoſes. Now, to wiſh to ſhake off theſe rules, which render government eaſy, conſiſtent, and popular, for the ſake of acting by mere will and humour,

mour, would be childish folly. but coolly to intend to ruin the liberties of the first people in the world; to destroy the talents and virtues, the arts and sciences, the power, the commerce, and the happiness of such a nation as this (for none of these can long survive our liberties), would be a work of much deeper guilt in this enlightened age, when those blessings are become greater in themselves, and the value of them is better known; than any of the tyrannical attempts which our forefathers so bravely withstood. I am firmly persuaded that I speak the language of our sovereign's heart, when I say, there is no person in the whole extent of his dominions, so strongly interested in the preservation of our liberties as himself. To destroy them would be to pluck up the roots of his own greatness; to become the inconsiderable monarch of a wretched people.

many titles of pre-eminence above other nations, is the higheft office in value and dignity which can fall to the lot of man. It opens, to a generous mind, the nobleft, the greateft, the moft practicable means of ferving our country, and doing the moft extenfive good to our fellow-creatures. Great part of the work is made eafy to them by a conftitution of government, and a fyftem of laws, which carry with them the experience and wifdom of ages; fuch as the moft comprehenfive mind of itfelf could never have invented, and would chufe to be reftrained by; but, indeed, they are not properly reftraints, but the rules which wifdom and goodnefs have formed to themfelves, for the execution of their own purpofes. Now, to wifh to fhake off thefe rules, which render government eafy, confiftent, and popular, for the fake of acting by mere will and humour,

mous, would be childish folly: but coolly to intend to ruin the liberties of the first people in the world, to destroy the talents and virtues, the arts and sciences, the power, the commerce, and the happiness of such a nation as this (for none of these can long survive our liberties), would be a work of much deeper guilt in this enlightened age, when those blessings are become greater in themselves, and the value of them is better known, than any of the tyrannical attempts which our forefathers so bravely withstood. I am firmly persuaded that I speak the language of our sovereign's heart, when I say, there is no person in the whole extent of his dominions, so strongly interested in the preservation of our liberties as himself. To destroy them would be to pluck up the roots of his own greatness; to become the inconsiderable monarch of a wretched people.

ple. This is a truth which has received new light and evidence from the experience of every reign, has actually rendered the revival of arbitrary designs more odious and more impracticable, and it ought to render us very cautious of imputing such designs to those who are appointed to rule over us. How cruel and ungrateful must such suspicions appear to him, who places his happiness in the love of his people! Men of virtue and moderation will not indulge a disposition of mind so repugnant to prudence and humanity, and so destructive of happiness. They will think it not too late to show resentment, when they begin to feel oppression. What else is wanting, but union and public confidence to make us enjoy completely, the fullest tide of prosperity that ever flowed in upon any land?

There would be a manifest impropriety

in treating a subject of such universal concern, if I should entirely omit to consider, in what respects it is applicable to that illustrious order, whose commands I am now obeying. Let it therefore be allowed me, with all due humility and respect, not as an officious adviser, but as performing a part of my office, to remind those who are the first in rank and titles among an active, knowing, and victorious people; that this pre-eminence was annexed to their birth, not by any natural right (for nature knows nothing of such distinctions), but to reward the merits of their ancestors, and to form an order in the state, whose property and education, by rendering them able and independent, might qualify them to be trusted with a perpetual share in the legislature. Now, in whatever hands power is lodged under a government so equitably constituted as ours; and indeed

under

under any government, there always goes along with it an obligation to use it to those purposes of public good, for which it appears to have been given. This is the only good tenure by which all legal authority is held. And while they feel themselves thus strictly obliged to acquire and exercise the virtues and the abilities, which are requisite to the discharge of their office; let them remember, that they are placed by their rank, as it were, in the public view; exposed to the examination of a people, who are more inclined to discover faults, than to forgive them. Not only their parliamentary conduct, but the abuse of their wealth and influence, the vicious, illiberal, or effeminate turn of their pleasures, even the idleness and amusements of their private hours, become matter of public curiosity and censure. Now, these are censures which the wise and good will always respect;

spect; and which the most rich and powerful cannot despise with impunity. Indeed, there is no rank of men, either in this or any other country, to whom it is of so much importance to maintain a good character; that treasure of life, the value of which is too little known; and without which eloquence, knowledge, and application, often become pernicious, and even contemptible qualities. Mere expence and magnificence can neither give it, nor atone for the want of it. The loss of weight and authority in one great council, can never be well supplied by procuring an undue influence over another: for neither God nor man will consent, that true honour and credit shall be attainable by any other expedients than wisdom and integrity.

Quitting therefore party and family connections, which engage the good and the bad indiscriminately in the defence of each others conduct, and whose interests, in some respects at least, must necessarily vary from that of the public; let every one pursue the plain open path of duty and honour, and let all unite in one virtuous confederacy to procure the good of the whole. And to enable them to render the important service they owe to their country, let them, at least, keep pace with the public improvement in every liberal branch of knowledge; let them exercise, in their private lives, that œconomy that preserves virtue, and that liberality which gives reputation; let them acquire habits of temperance and application, which alone can qualify men for great undertakings, and let them preserve that contempt of luxury, and firmness of mind, which can bear the loss of favour or of popularity. For indeed, without a

generous

generous indifference for the common objects of ambition, which nothing but a true sense of our religious duties can give, it will be extremely difficult for them, amidst the fluctuations of power and fortune, to maintain either integrity or peace of mind.

And now, may the all-wise Protector of empires enable his favoured people, in this their day of trial, to resume that prudence and temper; that steady, moderate, and generous spirit, which has carried them with success and honour through the dangers and commotions of former ages: so shall the terrors that afflict, and the calamities that threaten us, pass away like a cloud. Moved by the sense of impending evils, may they seek for refuge and support in the practice of their holy, and wise, and useful religion, which has efficacy to perfect all their improvements,

provements, and to correct the diforders they complain of; that one thing needful, and that one thing to them particularly wanting. May they ftill be diftinguifhed above other nations, and employed in executing the nobleft purpofes of Providence on this earthly ftage. " May knowledge and wifdom ftill be the ftability of their times;" and may they hold forth to the inftruction of mankind, a lafting example of freedom, virtue, and happinefs.

# SERMON

PREACHED BEFORE THE

INCORPORATED SOCIETY

FOR THE

*Propagation of the Gospel in Foreign Parts;*

AT THEIR

ANNIVERSARY MEETING

IN THE

PARISH CHURCH OF ST MARY-LE BOW,

On FRIDAY, February 19, 1773.

# SERMON, &c.

### Luke, Chap. ii. Ver. 14.

*Glory be to God in the highest, and on earth peace, good-will towards men.*

I KNOW no passage in the holy Scriptures, that may be adapted with more propriety to our present meeting, than this declaration from the angel of the gracious purposes of Heaven in publishing the Gospel. That which was the design of the Gospel itself must necessarily be the chief object of a Society instituted to propagate it. The generous office, we have undertaken, is, by instructing distant countries in religious truths, to promote the peace and happiness of mankind. It is by such actions the holy Scriptures allow the sons of men to consider themselves as glorifying God; and such, we are assured, are the most likely to obtain his favour and goodwill to men. Without entering into a farther explication of the words, suffer me to desire that you will keep in your minds the general principle contained in them; and you will find it easily applicable to the facts, the circumstances, and the different situations of things, which I shall take leave to mention, as being more or less connected with the credit and influence of this Society.

The first object of our zeal was the conversion of the Indians; and it should seem no difficult task to influence the minds of men, who have few religious notions of their own growth, and appear to have no ftrong prejudices in favour of them. Such minds one would think might eafily be led to receive a religion of the moft fimple form, confifting of a few great luminous principles, and inculcating plain rules of life and conduct, which muft approve their ufefulnefs in deferts, as well as in cities. Such doctrines, founded on Divine authority, would, in all appearance, be particularly welcome, where the reftraints of law and government have but little force. Yet it has happened contrary to our hopes, that the preaching of the Gofpel has been of fmall efficacy amongft the Indians. The fagacity, for which they are remarkable, feems to be of a partial kind, and to partake more of inftinct than of reafon. They can employ great art to obtain their ends; to procure what they defire; or to gain a fuperiority over an enemy: but their paffions sions and habits proceeding always in one narrow track, they have neither relish nor discernment for the clearest truths, to which they have not been accustomed. After shewing the greatest address and courage in subduing or surprising an enemy, they cannot comprehend that it would be generous not to torture him, and that it would be wise to give such treatment as they would wish to receive. They have besides an untameable savage spirit, which has refused to hear the voice of instruction; which has obstinately rejected the arts and improvements of the Europeans, and has hitherto only adopted the most beastly of their vices.

For these reasons, though we ought not to remit our endeavours, yet I fear we have little reason to hope for their conversion, till some great change in their manners has made them abandon their savage vagrant

vagrant life, and prepared them for the discipline of law and religion.

But a more promising field is opened to our hopes, in the populous provinces of our own colonies. The rapid increase of their numbers on every side, in a country where the means of subsistence are easy, and open, together with the perpetual accession of inhabitants from Europe, are continually forming new congregations. Now knowledge of all kinds will probably be rare amongst men who are entering into the first rudiments of society; and while their attention is bent on procuring the necessaries of life, it is not to be expected that they should be either diligent or succefsful in the improvement of religious knowledge. Here therefore the instructions that are conveyed to them by the liberality of this Society, may be of essential and durable service. This is

sowing

sowing the good seed in a fruitful soil; and what is so planted may produce returns of an hundred fold, and afford fruit and nourishment to future generations. Allow me to indulge a little the pleasure of contemplating in prospect the good that may result in after-times from this our labour of love.

Perhaps the annals of history have never afforded a more grateful spectacle to a benevolent and philosophic mind, than the growth and progress of the British colonies in North America. We see a number of scattered settlements, formed at first for the purposes of trade, or from a spirit of enterprize, to procure a maintenance, or to enjoy the exercise of their religion, which in those unhappy days was refused them at home, growing by degrees, under the protection of their mother-country, who treated them with the indulgence due to their weakness and infancy, into little separate commonwealths. Placed in a climate, that soon became fruitful and healthy by their industry; possessing that liberty which was the natural growth of their own country, and secured by her power against foreign enemies, they seem to have been intended, as a solitary experiment, to instruct the world to what improvements and happiness mankind will naturally attain, when they are suffered to use their own prudence, in search of their own interest. I must repeat it again, as an observation not unworthy of this audience and this occasion, that there is no instance in the records of time, where infant colonies have been treated with such a just and liberal indulgence.

Had these settlements been left to shift for themselves, they would have perished and been swept away by the rough course of accidents, like feeds that are scattered by the winds, of which not one in a thousand takes root and comes to maturity. Had they been planted by any kingdom but our own, the inhabitants would have carried with them the chains and oppression, to which they had been inured at home. they would have been subject to the schemes of ministers and favourites, and have suffered more from their ignorance than from their rapine. At best they could only have hoped to be considered as the live stock upon a lucrative farm, which might sometimes be suffered to thrive for the sake of its produce.

But Britain from the beginning has treated her colonies in a very different manner. She has not sold them her protection at the price of their liberty: she has always been ready to encourage their industry

industry, to relieve their wants, and to revenge their injuries; and has fought no other advantage from so generous a conduct, but the mutual benefit arising to distant countries from the supply of each other's wants. Adhering to these maxims, she has continued to reap the fruits of her own wisdom and moderation in a surprising encrease of national greatness, while her prosperous colonies are spreading without interruption over a vast continent, that may in a few centuries rival the commerce, the arts, and the power of Europe.

It is difficult for man to look into the destiny of future ages. The designs of Providence are too vast and complicated, and our own powers are too narrow, to admit of much satisfaction to our curiosity. But when we see many great and powerful causes constantly at work.

work, we cannot doubt of their producing proportionable effects. The colonies in North America have not only taken root and acquired strength, but seem hastening with an accelerated progress to such a powerful state, as may introduce a new and important change in human affairs. Descended from ancestors of the most improved and enlightened part of the old world, they receive as it were by inheritance all the improvements and discoveries of their mother-country. And it happens fortunately for them to commence their flourishing state at a time when the human understanding has attained to the free use of its powers, and has learned to act with vigour and certainty. They may avail themselves not only of the experience and industry, but even of the errors and mistakes of former days. Let it be considered for how many ages great part of the world

appears

appears not to have thought at all; how many more they have been bufied in forming fyftems and conjectures; while reafon has been loft in a labyrinth of words, and they never feem to have fufpected, on what frivolous matters their minds were employed. And let it be well underftood, what rapid improvements, what important difcoveries have been made in a few years, by a few countries, with our own at their head, which have at laft difcovered the right method of ufing their faculties. May we not reafonably expect that a number of provinces, poffeffed of thefe advantages, and quickened by mutual emulation, with only the common progrefs of the human mind, fhould very confiderably enlarge the boundaries of fcience? The vaft continent itfelf, over which they are gradually fpreading, may be confidered as a treafure, yet untouched, of natural productions, that shall hereafter afford ample matter for commerce and contemplation. And if we reflect what a stock of knowledge may be accumulated by the constant progress of industry and observation, fed with fresh supplies from the stores of nature, assisted sometimes by those happy strokes of chance, which mock all the powers of invention, and sometimes by those superior characters, which arise occasionally to instruct and enlighten the world, it is difficult even to imagine to what height of improvement their discoveries may extend.

And perhaps they may make as considerable advances in the arts of civil government and the conduct of life.

We have reason to be proud, and even jealous, of our excellent constitution. But those equitable principles on which it was formed, an equal representation,

(the

(the best discovery of political wisdom) and a just and commodious distribution of power, which with us were the price of civil wars, and the reward of the virtues and sufferings of our ancestors, descend to them as a natural inheritance, without toil or pain. But must they rest here as in the utmost effort of human genius? Can chance and time, the wisdom and the experience of publick men, suggest no new remedy against the evils, their vices and ambition are perpetually apt to cause? May they not hope, without presumption, to preserve a greater zeal for piety and publick devotion than we have done? For sure it can hardly happen to them, as it has to us, that when religion is best understood and rendered most pure and reasonable, that then should be the precise time, when many cease to believe and practise it, and all in general become

become moſt indifferent to it. May they not poſſibly be more ſucceſsful than their mother-country has been, in preſerving that reverence and authority, which is due to the laws? to thoſe who make, and to thoſe who execute them? May not a method be invented of procuring ſome tolerable ſhare of the comforts of life to thoſe inferior uſeful ranks of men, to whoſe induſtry we are indebted for the whole? Time and diſcipline may diſcover ſome means to correct the extreme inequalities of condition between the rich and the poor, ſo dangerous to the innocence and the happineſs of both. They may fortunately be led by habit and choice to deſpiſe that luxury, which is conſidered with us as the true enjoyment of wealth. They may have little reliſh for that ceaſeleſs hurry of amuſements, which is purſued in this country without pleaſure,

exerciſe,

exercise, or employment. And perhaps after trying some of our follies and caprices, and rejecting the rest, they may be led by reason and experiment to that old simplicity, which was first pointed out by nature, and has produced those models which we still admire in arts, eloquence, and manners. The diversity of new scenes and situations, which so many growing states must necessarily pass through, may introduce changes in the fluctuating opinions and manners of men, which we can form no conception of. And not only the gracious disposition of Providence, but the visible preparation of causes, seems to indicate strong tendencies towards a general improvement.

And I hope that these matters, which I have presumed to dwell upon perhaps a little too minutely, will not appear totally foreign to the present occasion, if we reflect to whatever limits the population of our colonies may extend, whatever ſtates and kingdoms they may form, through all the progreſs of their fortunes and proſperity, the labours of this Society will probably continue to operate with an increaſing influence. That ſober and reaſonable ſenſe of duty, which has been taught under our direction to a few ſcattered villages, may give its character hereafter to the religion and morals of a powerful ſtate. The weak and imperfect fruits we reap at preſent may bear no higher proportion to the future benefits that may ariſe, than that of a few ſcattered ſeeds to the fulneſs of the harveſt.

And perhaps the diſintereſted zeal of this Society for the inſtruction of our brethren in North America, may tend to revive that union and cordiality between the mother-country and its colonies,

which

which for the common utility ought never to have been interrupted. It is by no means decent from this place to cenfure the conduct of our fuperiors, or even to fuppofe it blameable, but furely as good fubjects we may wifh and endeavour to heal the wounds of our country, without enquiring by what hand they were inflicted. We may, and I think we ought to wifh, that the true intereft of the whole extenfive community may govern our future contefts, and regulate all our claims. Our mutual relation was formed, and has hitherto fubfifted, by a perpetual communication of benefits. We want the produce of foils and climates, that differ fo much from our own, and they will long have occafion for the fruits of our arts, our induftry, and our experience. And fhould they ever ceafe to want our protection, which as long as we render it be-

neficial

neficial to them they never will; yet we may still continue united in interest, in commerce, and the grateful remembrance of old services. May the wise and good on both sides, without enquiring too curiously into the grounds of past animosities, endeavour by all prudent means to restore that old publick friendship and confidence, which made us great, happy, and victorious. To countries so closely united it is needless, and even dangerous, to have recourse to the interpretation of charters and written laws. Such discussions excite jealousy, and intimate an unfriendly disposition. It is common utility, mutual wants and mutual services, that should point out the true line of submission and authority. Let them respect the power that saved them; and let us always love the companions of our dangers and our glories. If we consider their prosperity as making

part

part of our own, we shall feel no jealousy at their improvements, and they will always cheerfully submit to an authority, which they find is exercised invariably to the common advantage. During all our happy days of concord, partly from our national moderation, and partly from the wisdom, and sometimes perhaps from the carelessness of our ministers, they have been trusted in a good measure with the intire management of their affairs: and the success they have met with ought to be to us an ever memorable proof, that the true art of government consists in not governing too much. And why should friendship and gratitude, and long attachments, which inspire all the relish and sweetness of private life, be supposed to be of no weight in the intercourse between great communities? These are principles of human nature, which act

with

with much greater certainty on numbers than on individuals. If properly cultivated, they may to us be productive of the noblest benefits; and, at all events, will neither lessen the extent of our power, nor shorten the duration of it.

When things are on so reasonable a footing, if there should happen to be any errors in government, they will soon be corrected by the friendly disposition of the people, and the endeavours to separate the interest of the colonies from that of Great Britain will be received with the indignation that is due to the artifices of factious men, who wish to grow eminent by the misfortunes of their country.

Even in that future state of independency, which some amongst them ignorantly wish for, but which for their true interest can never be too long delayed; the old and prudent will often look back on their present happiness with regret; and consider the peace and security, the state of visible improvement, and brotherly equality, which they enjoyed under the protection of their mother-country, as the true golden age of America.

I need not suggest how favourable these dispositions must prove to the reception of the religious and benevolent doctrines, which it is the business of this society to propagate. Under a mutual inclination to peace and good-will, the lessons of piety we teach will be heard with that fair attention which always turns to the advantage of truth, and the claims we make will be estimated (which is all we ought to desire) by the reasonableness of them.

I own I feel upon my mind a strong impression of the public advantages that would result from this benevolent and christian policy; and I could wish for the

*interest*

interest of mankind, and of our country in particular, that it may not be thought wholly of a visionary nature. I think I can see a strong and immediate demand upon us for such a conduct, from the situation we are in, and the unusual occurrences that have passed before us within a few years. There seems at present to be a great and general commotion, and tendency to change, in the minds of men. Animated by the gradual improvement of knowledge, and the fortunate example of this country, our neighbours have had the courage to think with greater freedom on the most important subjects, and to look for something better in religion and government, than they find established among themselves. And even in this land of liberty, where we have been long in possession of the most solid and valuable truths, the spirit of enquiry is still at work,

work, and urging its purfuits with a dangerous freedom, that rifks more than it can hope to gain At the fame time not only difcontent and faction, but the real difficulties of things, the extent, the fluctuation and the intricacies of commerce, afford fufficient exercife for political wifdom. Add to this a vaft acceffion of diftant territory, the art of governing which we are yet to learn. Our colonies are rifing into ftates and nations. The extreme boundaries of the world are opening to our view, and regions, unknown to our fathers, may foon become the objects of contention. In this great fhifting fcene of human affairs, the concerns of this extenfive empire are growing every year into more importance and dignity. It behoves us to adopt fome plan of conduct, that fhall be fuitable to our fituation and the high character we fuftain. The intereft of of Britain, considered singly by itself, ought not at present to be the sole, and in a few ages may not be the most considerable object of attention. We have already tried what advantage is to be found in governing by force, and have no reason to be proud of the experiment. What benefit has accrued to the public from the plunder and desolation of an industrious, helpless people? The whole profit we have reaped from so much injustice and dishonour, has ended in fraudulent schemes, vain and extravagant expectations, ruinous expence and luxury, attended with a general loss of credit and confidence, a sudden suspension of commerce and industry, and an almost total stoppage of the main springs and vital motions of society. It requires no common degree of wisdom to deliver our country from such gains and such prosperity as this!

A great

A great liberal commanding spirit is wanting; such as has appeared but rarely in modern times, but was better known to the ancients, which, without computing and calculating what is strictly due, can extort affection and gratitude by public services, which can sacrifice little and even great interests to the establishment of a solid permanent authority, founded on justice and moderation· which permitting its subjects to enjoy and improve all their natural advantages, can always avail itself of their wealth and numbers, for the defence or the glory of the empire; and is sure to find the most powerful resources of government in their friendship and love.

We presume not to instruct our rulers in the measures of government. but it is the proper office of a preacher of the gospel of peace, to point out the laws of justice and equity, which must ultimately regulate

regulate the happiness of states as well as of individuals; and which are no other in effect than those benevolent christian morals which it is the province of this society to teach, transferred from the duties of private life to the administration of public affairs. In fact, by what bond of union shall we hold together the members of this great empire, dispersed and scattered as they lie over the face of the earth? No power can be swift or extensive enough to answer the purpose. Some art must be employed to interest all the distant parts in the preservation of the whole, which can only be effected by serving, obliging, and protecting them. It ought not to be the first object in contemplation, what we are to get by them, but how we can best improve, assist, and reward them; by what benefits we may procure their happiness and win their affection. But is government

government, then, entitled to no emoluments in recompence for all its cares? I answer, that they who have the heart to do good to those who depend upon them, will always meet with ample return. None are so sure to reap the benefits of the soil, as they who have spared no expence in the cultivation. And it is universally true, that the more we exact from our subjects, the less we shall gain from them. " BOUNTIFULNESS IS A PLENTIFUL GARDEN, AND MERCIFULNESS ENDURETH FOR EVER." Let the distant nations, that depend upon us, be made to know and feel that they owe their peace and happiness to our protection. Let them be encouraged to consider themselves not as our slaves, but as our friends and brethren. And let us endeavour to wipe away the tears from the poor oppressed natives of India; and suffer them, if possible, to enjoy some taste of the legal security and civil liberty, which renders life dear to ourselves, which are blessings hitherto unknown to those climates, but more grateful to the heart of man, than all the fruits and odours which nature has lavished upon them.

This righteousness and mercy, which is due to all men, but especially to those who are under our protection, is the law of nature, the command of religion, and it ought to be the first and leading maxim of civil policy. But it is amazing how slowly in all countries the principles of natural justice, which are so evidently necessary in private life, has been admitted into the administration of public affairs. Not many ages ago, it was customary to engage in war without a reasonable cause or provocation, and to carry it on without humanity or mercy. Since then, it is

happily

happily become necessary for states to explain their motives, and justify their conduct, before they begin to destroy their fellow-creatures. And blessed be his memory who first taught the soldier to spare the useful husbandman, and to feel a horror at the shedding of innocent blood.

It has been the policy of government, such as it is, from the earliest times, to keep distant provinces and colonies under the most severe restraints and subjection. Yet when those restraints have been removed, the mother-country has always been a great gainer by the advantages she has communicated to her subjects. Indeed it is a truth, not more important than it is evident and obvious, that the most sure and effectual method of receiving good from men is to do good to them, or, as St. Paul beautifully expresses it, "TO

PROVOKE ONE ANOTHER TO GOOD WORKS." But the minds of men are not sufficiently prepared and enlightened by experience to adopt it in practice. A time, I doubt not, will come, in the progressive improvement of human affairs, when the checks and restraints we lay on the industry of our fellow-subjects, and the jealousies we conceive at their prosperity, will be considered as the effects of a mistaken policy, prejudicial to all parties, but chiefly to ourselves. It would be a noble effort of virtuous ambition to anticipate this discovery, to break through the prejudices and selfish spirit of the age, to find a better path to our true interest, and to make our country great, and powerful, and rich, not by force or fraud, but by justice, friendship, and humanity.

I should not have dwelt so long on so unusual a subject, had it not been for the great and almoſt infinite importance of it. The virtue of a private man aſſiſts and supports a few individuals, but this public virtue does good to thouſands and tens of thouſands. The former relieves the diſtreſs of a friend, or of a family. the latter acts in a higher ſphere; it founds ſtates and kingdoms, or makes them proſperous and happy. Yet all this merit, which a nation can never ſufficiently acknowledge, at leaſt all that we preſume to deſcribe, conſiſts in the right application of the plain good rules, which are ſo often repeated to us in ſcripture, " WHATSOEVER YE WOULD THAT MEN SHOULD DO UNTO YOU, DO YE EVEN SO UNTO THEM. FOLLOW THAT WHICH IS GOOD TO ALL MEN. LOOK NOT EVERY MAN ON HIS OWN THINGS, BUT EVERY MAN ALSO ON THE THINGS OF OTHERS. BEAR YE ONE ANOTHER'S BURTHENS, AND SO FULFIL

THE LAW OF CHRIST". But these truths lie before the eye of men, like the medicinal herbs in the open field; and for want of applying them to their proper objects, they remain ignorant of their virtues. Yet, we may say, with a pious confidence, that this has not been our own case. This Society has thought that we could not obey these divine precepts in a manner more agreeable to the true spirit of them, than by teaching to distant nations the truths that are best calculated to make them happy. Could we teach them to the great and the wife of this world, that would be happiness indeed, that would be the most effectual and the most beneficial propagation of the gospel, that the world has yet seen. Mankind would then have an experimental proof of the salvation offered to us from above; and

would

would acknowledge, with gratitude, the propriety of that meſſage from Heaven, "Glory be to God in the highest, on earth peace, goodwill towards men."

A

# SERMON

PREACHED IN THE

PARISH-CHURCH OF CHRIST CHURCH,

LONDON,

On Thursday, April the 24th, 1777.

Being the Time of the YEARLY MEETING of the CHILDREN Educated in the CHARITY-SCHOOLS in and about the Cities of LONDON and WEST-MINSTER.

# SERMON, &c.

PROVERBS xxii. part of the 6th verse.

*Train up a child in the way he should go—*

IT is unnecessary before such an audience as this to speak of the importance of a good education: but to point out that which is best, to mark the steps by which we should train up a child in the way he should go, is matter of use and difficulty. But the subject at present before us is of a narrower kind, and is confined to that lowest species, and, as it were, rudiments of education, which is suited to the children of the poor in their earliest days. In the greatest part of this, too, I have been happily

pily anticipated by the valuable performances of those who have gone before me in this office, and which lie before the eye of the public. They have considered the groundless objections, and they and the Society have profited by the reasonable ones that have been made against the institutions that have been adopted.

It were to be wished, indeed, that through better laws and principles and habits than at present obtain amongst us, the lowest of our fellow-subjects were so far removed from distress as to be able to maintain and educate their own children. For it must be owned, that all the care and instruction which public charity can purchase for them, are but very imperfect substitutes for the tenderness and attention of honest parents.

However, as things are at present circumstanced, it is the office of good men, as stewards of the manifold grace of God, to supply the defects of the careless, the profligate, and the distressed part of their species. They have the melancholy honour to find that their virtues arise from the faults and miseries of their fellow-creatures. Their labour at present is much increased by the apparent necessity of such services as these, but even at present that labour is not without its reward, and it rests in hope of a more suitable and immortal recompence hereafter.

There is one objection against the institution we think it our duty to patronize, which has made an impression upon the minds of men, that is not yet worn out. It is, that some part at least of the instructions provided by us are unnecessary, and even prejudical to the lower ranks of life, by giving a taste for enjoyments, and a sense of their ownmerit, superior to the

offices

offices they must be employed in. That there are kinds of knowledge and instruction, which would be very unsuitable to their low station, is readily admitted. And it is no less true, that it would be neither just nor wise to leave them entirely destitute of all instruction. But it is evident that the nature and quantity of the instruction necessary to be given, is to be determined by the demands of the age and the society they live in. There have been times of ignorance and barbarism, when princes and their great officers of state were unable to write, and sometimes even to read. But then this ignorance was in a manner general, and the bad effects of it appeared in the coarse and corrupt manners of the people, who were held in a shameful dependence on one order of men, who had monopolized the little knowledge that was then to be met with, and, like

other

other monopolizers, they were indifferent about the goodneſs of their merchandize, and took care not to overſtock the market. But in a country like this, which is ſo much indebted for its wealth, its power, and its happineſs, to its improvements in knowledge, it is ſurely requiſite, that inſtruction ſhould be diffuſed amongſt the lower orders of men in a more liberal meaſure. Even the ſervices we expect from them require, on many occaſions, a degree of prudence which cannot be attained without ſome education. The progreſs we have made in arts and commerce has raiſed a greater demand for ſkill and judgment in the meaneſt of our workmen. And however backward we may be to acknowledge the relation, yet reaſon and religion agree to tell us, that the poor are our brethren. It does not become us to widen and aggravate the little differences
that

that fortune has placed between us. Nor is it just or wise, with regard to the public, to deprive it of the benefits it has often received from the useful and vigorous talents that have been nursed up in the hardiness of poverty. As for the public mischiefs that are to be apprehended from trusting the poor with too much knowledge, as far as we can judge from experience, the danger is imaginary. It is not from their knowledge, but from their idleness and their ignorance, and the bad example of their superiors, that such mischiefs are to be apprehended. But whatever kind of knowledge it may be thought proper to deny the poor, one kind there is (and the consideration of it is at present our chief concern) which all must allow to be expedient for them, and that is the knowledge of their duty. They who are the most rigorous to the poor

poor in this world, will certainly not grudge them the hopes of a better life.

Now to propagate this useful knowledge is the great object of our Society, and we have certainly contributed very confiderably to fo good a work, by diftributing printed copies of the bible and our excellent liturgy, either gratis, or at fo low a price as comes within the reach of the poor; and by fupplying them with manuals of devotion, and many practical treatifes, of which we have certainly chofen by far the beft of the kind.

It is unpleafant to cenfure the performances of men, whofe good intentions deferve juft commendation, but it is alfo incumbent upon us to provide that our own good intentions may not lofe their effect by any error or imperfection in the performance. Let it therefore be allowed me, not from a fpirit of criticifm, but as repeating the complaints of the beft and wifeft men, and I flatter myfelf the fenfe of many of my hearers, to obferve, that thefe tracts of piety and devotion are frequently written with great want of judgment. They certainly have not the fuccefs that might be expected, either in forming the underftandings, or mending the lives of the few that ufe them. What are the caufes of this difappointment is an enquiry that deferves to employ a little of our time

It is impoffible to explain by how many different ways men may depart from the rule of their duty. There is one fimple and uniform line of truth, but the deviations of ignorance and error are infinite. Yet amidft all this variety I may venture to fingle out one great and leading principle which appears to me to have contributed very largely to thefe injudicious compofitions. It is the opinion that the

fole

sole intention of our religion is to prepare its followers for a better life, without any immediate regard to their happiness at present. This was one of the earliest and primitive sources of error, when christianity first began to suffer by the contagion of that superstition and false philosophy, which it was intended to extirpate. To an attentive observer of human nature and the world we live in, it must necessarily appear to be the intention of our creator, which to us is the strongest of all laws, that all men should concur in procuring that happiness which every man wishes for, and which every man has an equal capacity to acquire and an equal right to expect. But the misfortune is, that men are not contented to purchase happiness at the only price at which it can be had, but hope, by a foolish kind of cunning, to obtain the end without using the natural means.

means. It is thus they seek for health without temperance, for knowledge and wealth without industry, and for religion and happiness without virtue. To encourage these wild pursuits it was maintained very early that the gospel was an institution designed only to lead us to Heaven. The immediate consequence was, that many well meaning men retired not only from the business and vanities, but from the duties of the present life, and consumed themselves in solitude and useless austerities; giving their prayers only to the world, which wanted their good offices and assistance. It would be tedious and unnecessary to show what advantages were taken, after the true grounds of religion were weakened or rendered uncertain, by designing men, of the simplicity of their brethren. To do that would be to enter into the history of the growth and progress of the papal

pal power, which reduced mankind to a state of general ignorance and servitude, from whence the greatest part of Europe is but just beginning to recover. And even in this favoured country, where we have so long enjoyed that religious liberty, which all have a right to, yet the same principle still continues to operate, weakly and silently indeed, but not imperceptibly. The shortest way to judge of its influence, and to discern its effects, is to compare it with the scripture-rule of our duty. In the first place it is observable that what is there required of us is never laid down in a very methodical or circumstantial manner. We do not think justly of our holy religion, unless we remember that it is the most extensive and universal of all religious dispensations. It is not only revealed, but it is adapted to every country and every climate, to all the different races of men, and to all the infinite forms of society and government in which they can be placed. Now it seems at first sight, that if there is a law of such universal and unbounded authority, it cannot possibly consist of all the innumerable rules, which are applicable to every particular case: it must rather be composed of a few great and luminous precepts, comprehending the general principles that are to govern our lives.

Now, this is the very form and method in which the gospel morals are delivered to us. Your own recollection will anticipate what I am going to say. Indeed it is hardly necessary to observe to you that the whole of our duty is declared by our great lawgiver to consist in the love of God and of our neighbour. To do unto other men as we would they should do unto us, we are told, by the same authority,

rity, is the law and the prophets. Let no man seek his own, but every man another's wealth. Follow that which is good to all men. By love serve one another, for love is the fulfilling of the law. These great and general principles are the true characteristics of a religion designed for the use and benefit of the whole world. And it is remarkable, that the sacred writers have seldom given us any particular or circumstantial views of duty. Some very important branches of it are but slightly mentioned, or alluded to, or left to be collected from the first principles themselves. And where particular duties are enjoined they are not described with exactness and precision. If we are commanded to obey our parents, or to relieve the poor, the nature and measure of that obedience and that relief must be determined not from the words of Scripture,

but

but from the wants and the conditions of the society we live in, the manners of the age, the sense and the expectations of good men, and the impression which objects then present ought to make upon reasonable minds. And thus without tying us down to minute instructions, the spirit of God governs us in a more liberal manner. He trusts the direction of our own conduct to the strength of our own minds and the integrity of our own hearts. Our duty is not prescribed to us by certain specific rules, but arises continually from the actions and business of human life. The circumstances of every situation we can be placed in will suggest to an upright mind the measures of its behaviour. Our obligation thus taking its rise from the situations and characters in which we act is something fixed and substantial, and at the same time, by the universality of its principles,

principles accommodates itself to all the changes in human affairs. And by mixing thus intimately in the springs and principles of action, it assumes a right to conduct and govern every scene of human life, and forms, as the exigencies of the world require, not only saints and martyrs, but princes and statesmen. The duty therefore of a good Christian does not banish him from the world, or entice him into some solitary path of life; it rather calls him into the midst of it, and prompts him to seek occasions of being greatly and extensively useful. This at least is the idea which we must form of our religion from reading the gospel itself. Christ himself was a fountain of benevolence that flowed without ceasing to supply the wants of mankind. The lives of the apostles and the first disciples were active and social, and spent in the service of the world; and

if

if they appear themselves to have been more excellent and valuable than the common race of men, it is only because they were employed in a sublimer species of usefulness.

As far therefore as any religious treatise departs from this character of Christian duty, so far it tends to mislead the mind, and frustrate the good purposes it was intended to serve. Faith and devotion are the surest guides and strongest incentives to virtuous actions, but that author would strip them of their noblest merit who should represent them as resting in mere contemplation, or as matters totally distinct from, and unconnected with the rest of our duty. And whatever tends to divert our attention from the services we owe to our neighbour, or to lessen the importance of them, or to substitute any other branch of duty in its place, is so far defective,

fective, and injurious to the purity and simplicity of the Gospel. " The grace of God hath appeared from Heaven unto men, teaching us that, denying ungodliness and worldly lusts, we should live soberly, righteously, and godly in this present world." You see that the great Apostle of the Gentiles makes Revelation itself the handmaid to virtue. And let us remember that it is not only the inferior members of society, whose poverty and ignorance renders them the objects of our care, that are subject to this divine law: the higher men take their rank in the world, in proportion to the power and influence they acquire, they will find that their obligations are too enlarged. It is a work of no small thought and judgment, even to spend a large fortune with usefulness and propriety, to observe a just and liberal oeconomy without the imputation of avarice

rice or profusion; to comply with the manners and innocent customs, and yet shun the dissipation and vices of the age, and to reconcile our own inclinations and enjoyments with our character, our station, and the good of our countty. In such situations to perceive and to do the good we are capable of doing is a severe and serious task, and requires the whole attention of the strongest mind. But the public scenes of life are the true stage for piety and virtue to display themselves with the best advantage. There arise the great and noble opportunities for the sacrifice of pleasure and interest, there self-denial has a use and lustre that rewards all its sufferings, and there the benevolent mind is animated with the prospect of doing extensive good to multitudes, and of serving future generations.

The manner in which we now consider the

the duty of a Christian does not exclude or derogate in the least degree from the important truths which are revealed to us concerning the nature and the dispensations of God. All those truths are the improvement and continuation of the discoveries of reason. We acknowledge with veneration the influence they claim over our hearts and minds; but we confine ourselves at present to the consideration of their blessed effects visible in the lives of good men. The depth of the riches of the wisdom and mercy of God is exemplified in the gospel, not by methods of devotion and self-denial removed and separate from the common ways of life; but by instructing us as rational creatures to accommodate our minds with all godliness and honesty to the world we are placed in, and that part that is allotted to us. This method of treating our duty

opens

opens to us a rich and noble vein of thought. I shall venture to pursue it through a few of its consequences, at the risk of departing a little from the more immediate subject of my discourse.

If the practice of our religion consists in the love of our neighbour and our usefulness to society, this will furnish us with a very easy rule for the interpretation of those passages in Scripture that seem to be tinctured with unusual severity. They who are no friends to religion are apt to consider that self-denial, which it teaches, as an unreasonable precept, subjecting mankind to unnecessary sufferings, which in all appearance are neither suggested by interest nor enjoined by virtue. But when we learn that this and every other duty are only branches of that behaviour which consults the good of the whole, we then perceive that the self-denial required of us

must

must be always of such a kind as is neither unreasonable nor unnecessary. Indeed self-denial, in its full extent, is not merely a religious duty, but a condition annexed to the attainment of excellence in every kind. It is a law of nature and Providence that nothing great or valuable can be performed, without giving up many favourite amusements, pleasures, and prejudices. Self-denial seen in this light is so far from being useless, that it is the very discipline of Prudence in the conduct of life. It is a superior and a master virtue, and should not be debased to superficial and trifling austerities. When it ceases to be useful it becomes puerile and impertinent. The real scenes of life supply us with sufficient occasions for a rational and manly exercise of this virtue. Deny yourselves the gratifications that reason condemns, though they are recommended

mended by fashion and example. Sacrifice not your own judgment and your better inclinations to the imperious vanity of those who take the lead in folly, and see the world weak enough to follow them. Disdain the profits that are the fruits of fraud, rapine, or servility: and you will soon find that you must pay a considerable price for the satisfaction of acting an honest part. Thus the rule of doing good is the measure of every virtue.

Was humility to signify a general unqualified submission to all our fellow-creatures, it would not be easy to describe its use or limits. But if it is a branch of that general behaviour which respects the good of society, it immediately becomes clear and intelligible. For this humility arises from a sense that the meanest of our species are our fellow creatures, and that as Christians we are children and servants of the same God.

It

It is not a mean, servile character, which affects to to be contemptible, and is so; but it is seen in those quiet, unpretending dispositions, which men are pleased to converse and live with, and which gain more than others by claiming less. In high ranks it is the natural expression of a great and liberal mind. It is the true, innocent art, though little known, of winning affection, and governing reasonable creatures.

Our Saviour's language is, "Whoever will be great among you, let him be your servant." Is there any thing in human nature more noble and magnificent than this idea of humility?

Indeed the very essence of Christian duty must necessarily consist in doing good. For what is justice, if it does no good, but useless severity? and what are even mercy and charity, if they do no good, but weak indulgence and vain profusion?

fusion? Consider what sort of men the world is most in want of. Is it not the industrious and frugal tradesman, the upright magistrate, the honest and able statesman, the good parent, the good husband, the good citizen? Those who duly carry on the business of life are they who best perform its duties. Judge of the nature of virtue by the true and genuine effects of it.

Let me add, in the last place, that this notion of duty, which represents it as consisting in doing good, and being useful to our fellow-creatures, is not only adapted to our present state of pilgrimage upon earth; but the same law will probably govern our future existence, and may possibly extend to all the superior orders of intelligent beings. It is a most important and commanding principle, and seems, like attraction, to pervade the whole universe.

verse. For sure we ought to reject, with a pious indignation, the fancy that we are to pass eternal days in listening to concerts of divine harmony, or in the indolent contemplation of our own happiness. Such imaginations favour too much of selfishness and sensuality. Look round all the compass of nature, and see if God has permitted any being to make itself happy by doing nothing and caring only for itself. In the immense extent of creation new scenes, new situations, new diversities of life and action, without end, will open themselves. But, sure, in all that extent God has not removed any set of his intelligent creatures beyond the limits and the operation of doing and receiving good. All nature is made perfect and happy by the support and assistance which its parts receive from each other. May we not be allowed to imagine, without presumption, that the exercise of this unlimited benevolence, of those tender mercies which are over all his works, is one great and everlasting source of happiness to the Deity himself? and may we not presume that God, who has indulged so large a share of that divine pleasure to us, who are perhaps the meanest of his offspring, has given a fuller measure of the same grace, and nobler exercises of that blessed employment which so much resembles his own, to those superior orders of spirits, that rise above us in all conceivable degrees of perfection.

On these suppositions it becomes clear and intelligible how the present life is a preparation for a better. Not only the good works we have done, and the rewards attending them, will follow us into the world of spirits, but the good principles we have learned, the good habits we have formed, the generous and benevolent passions

sions we have nourished and cultivated, will still make a part of our character, will accompany us into happier scenes, and still find their use and exercise. Our powers may be enlarged, our faculties may be improved, but still, in the most exalted station in the universe, the purest and most enlightened mind can find no employment more worthy of itself than that of doing good.

This, then, is the great ruling principle which ought to be ever present to our minds, and govern the whole conduct of our lives. In our most serious hours, and even in our amusements; whether we act ourselves, or pass a judgment on the actions or writings of other men, it will always be the certain test of what is right to enquire how fart his leading and sovereign principle has been attended to. This will help us, in a good measure, to distinguish and separate

rate the little blemishes which, through an indiscreet piety, are apt to steal into good men and good books.

I shall only add, that it is hardly possible for imagination to suggest a more perfect exercise of this heavenly principle, the true source of all human virtue, than the giving of due support and countenance to that excellent institution to which we are called by this day's solemnity.

FINIS.

Lightning Source UK Ltd.
Milton Keynes UK
UKHW030712120720
366376UK00004B/448